United Arab Emirates

United Arab Emirates

Peachtree

BY BARBARA A. SOMERVILL

Enchantment of the World™
Second Series

CHILDREN'S PRESS®

An Imprint of Scholastic Inc.

Frontispiece: **Dubai**

Consultant: Victoria Hightower, Assistant Professor of History, University of North Georgia, Dahlonega, GA

Please note: All statistics are as up-to-date as possible at the time of publication.

Book production by The Design Lab

Library of Congress Cataloging-in-Publication Data
Somervill, Barbara A.
 United Arab Emirates / by Barbara A. Somervill.
  pages cm — (Enchantment of the world)
 Includes bibliographical references and index.
 ISBN 978-0-531-23298-9 (library binding : alk. paper)
 1. United Arab Emirates—Juvenile literature. I. Title.
 DS247.T8S65 2016
 953.57—dc23   2015020051

1 2 3 4 5 6 7 8 9 10 R 25 24 23 22 21 20 19 18 17 16

Applying henna

Contents

Left to right: **Burj Khalifa, drinking tea, desert, Bedu, Emirati woman**

CHAPTER 1

A Desert Safari

EVERY AUTUMN, SAIF'S FATHER HEADS INTO THE desert with some of his sons. This year is Saif's first time to be included. Saif al-Khalifa al-Hamad was born in Dubai and has lived there all his life. He is a city boy, but his family traces its heritage back many generations to the days when there were no United Arab Emirates (UAE) and no cities on the Arabian Peninsula. Once, there were only the Bedouin, their camels, and some roughly traced trade routes in the desert sands.

Today is a different story. There are still plenty of camels, but there are also off-road, four-wheel-drive vehicles for crashing over sand dunes. There are wild gazelles browsing on wild grasses, and elegant resorts where wealthy tourists experience desert life in luxurious comfort. There are freshwater oases, ancient ghaf trees, and date palms. There are also highways and GPS tracking devices to prevent people from getting lost.

Opposite: **Men ride camels across the desert in Dubai. There are more than 350,000 camels in the United Arab Emirates.**

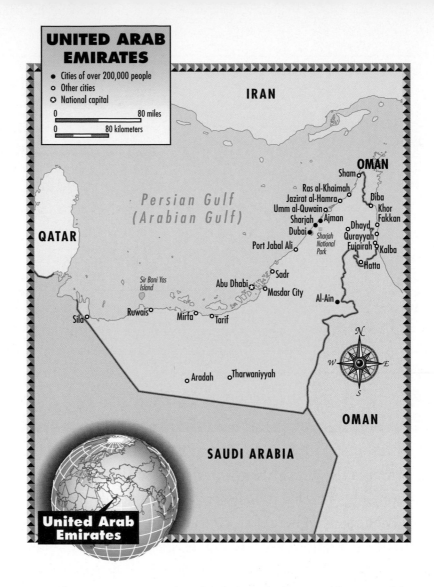

UNITED ARAB EMIRATES

- ● Cities of over 200,000 people
- ○ Other cities
- ⊕ National capital

0   80 miles

0   80 kilometers

IRAN

OMAN

Persian Gulf
(Arabian Gulf)

Sham

Ras al-Khaimah

Jazirat al-Hamra

Diba

Umm al-Quwain

Khor Fakkan

QATAR

Sharjah

Ajman

Dubai

Dhayd

Qurayyah

Sharjah National Park

Fujairah

Kalba

Port Jabal Ali

Hatta

Sir Bani Yas Island

Sadr

Abu Dhabi

Masdar City

Al-Ain

Ruwais

Sila

Mirfa

Tarif

Aradah

Tharwaniyyah

OMAN

SAUDI ARABIA

United Arab Emirates

This trip is just for Saif, his father, and two of his nine brothers. The family heads toward Liwa, an oasis on the northern edge of the Rub' al-Khali, better known as the Empty Quarter. In Liwa, Saif's family will meet up with Bedouin relatives who live nearby. Then, it is a camel ride into the desert for camping under the open sky. But first, there is dune bashing. Saif is excited about dune bashing, but a bit anxious about riding a camel.

Just over an hour away from Dubai, the family pulls off the road just before Al-Ain. The young men clamber into a four-wheel-drive vehicle driven by a professional desert safari guide. Saif's father is content to sit in the shade of a date palm and enjoy a cup of coffee and some conversation with other desert travelers.

Saif and his brothers are in for quite a ride. Dune bashing has several requirements for a successful adventure. The drivers let air out of their tires so the ride is spongy. They crank the music up until the vehicle vibrates. They push the gas pedal down as far as it will go. Dune bashing is like a roller coaster ride over shifting sands at impossibly steep angles. If

Dune bashing is a popular activity for Emiratis and tourists alike.

the passengers do not shriek, flinch, and shudder, the ride is not a success. The whiter the passengers' knuckles, the more satisfied drivers are that they earned their wages.

A lunch of barbecued goat, dates, and melon is served under a stand of acacias. The boys cannot stop talking about their reckless driver and how close they came to crashing. Would they do it again? Absolutely! Khalifa al-Hamad just rolls his eyes. He's glad his sons enjoyed themselves, but he is equally glad he did not have to join them dune bashing.

Tourists relax during an excursion into the desert of Dubai.

What's in a Name?

People in the United Arab Emirates have Arabic names. The naming system uses five name parts: *ism*, *kunya*, *nasab*, *laqab*, and *nisba*.

- An *ism* is the first name of the person, such as Sanya for a woman or Oumar for a man.
- A *kunya* is an honorific, a name that might refer to the person's firstborn son or it may be "aunt" or "uncle." Aunt or uncle does not mean a blood relative; it honors a person's age.
- The *nasab* refers to the person's father. *Bin* or *ibn* means "son of," and *bint* means "daughter of." Oumar bin Hassan means Oumar, the son of Hassan. A woman might be called Sanya bint Hassan, meaning Sanya, daughter of Hassan.
- The *laqab* is a nickname that highlights a good quality in a person. For example, Sanya bint Hassan al-Jamil means Sanya the beautiful, daughter of Hassan.
- The *nisba* describes a person's occupation, home region, or tribal heritage. Oumar bin Hassan al-Gergawi would be Oumar, son of Hassan from the family of Gergawi.

Knowing the parts of an Arabic name helps to understand both the people and their heritage.

Incredible Camels

The Arabic word for camel is *jamal*, which means "beauty," which is surprising because camels are not that beautiful. They do have a lot of interesting features, though. Camels can drink 40 gallons (150 liters) of water at one time. They can close their nostrils so that they don't breathe in sand during a sandstorm, and their legs can kick in all directions. Also, camels defend themselves by spitting nasty green stomach juices that stink. Watch out! They have great aim.

By the time the family reaches Liwa, it is almost dinnertime. Everyone washes up. The men pray in the front room; the women pray in a room off the kitchen. After prayers, it is time to eat. Khalifa and his cousin talk about family, friends, and even a bit of business.

The meal is delicious. The family feasts on roast camel meat, *al-jabab* bread, *harees* (a dish of ground wheat and chicken), dates, tomatoes, and hummus, with *luqaimat* (dumplings coated with sugar syrup) for dessert. There is prayer at Maghrib, just past 8:00 p.m. and again at 9:30 p.m. Then, it is time to sleep. Saif is concerned about riding a camel, but the others assure him that the camels are gentle and well trained.

Saif's family is up at dawn. They wash, pray, and eat. Khalifa double-checks the water supply, food rations, and safety equipment. Saif looks at his camel and grimaces. The camel looks back and spits a foul smelling wad of green yuck that lands inches from Saif's foot.

Khalifa and the boys mount up. Saif holds on for dear life, and his father tells him to relax.

By noon, the sun is high in the sky. The family stops on top of a huge dune and unrolls their prayer rugs. It is time to pray. The landscape is filled with rolling dunes, sparse grasses, and a deep blue sky. In the distance a four-wheel-drive vehicle rises up over a dune and then disappears.

"Once," says Khalifa with a sigh, "a Bedouin could ride a camel across this land for days and not see another person. Everything is changing."

"But, Father," says Saif, "the desert will always be here."

Khalifa smiles at his son, *"Insha'allah, Saif.* God willing."

The tallest dunes in the UAE rise about 400 feet (120 meters) from the desert floor.

CHAPTER 2

On the Arabian Peninsula

THE UNITED ARAB EMIRATES (UAE) IS A JAGGED triangle of land at the tip of the Arabian Peninsula, in southwestern Asia. Saudi Arabia lies to the south, and Oman runs along the UAE's eastern border. The Persian Gulf, also called the Arabian Gulf, forms most of the northern border, and the Gulf of Oman lies to the east.

The UAE is made up of seven emirates. Abu Dhabi is the largest, occupying 87 percent of the UAE. Abu Dhabi is mainly desert, but also includes about twenty-five islands in the Persian Gulf. Dubai, the second-largest emirate, has a natural port. Sharjah, just north of Dubai is mostly a coastal emirate. The smaller emirates are Ajman, Umm al-Quwain, Ras al-Khaimah, and Fujairah, the only emirate on the Gulf of Oman.

Opposite: **White sand beaches, large harbors, and fancy hotels line the coast of Dubai.**

Geographic Features of the United Arab Emirates

Area: 32,278 square miles (83,600 sq km)

Largest City: Dubai

Highest Elevation: Mount Yibir, 5,010 feet (1,527 m) above sea level

Lowest Elevation: Sea level along the coast

Length of Coastline: 819 miles (1,318 km)

Longest River: There are no rivers.

Largest Nature Preserve: Sir Bani Yas

Average High Temperature: In Dubai, 75°F (24°C) in January, 105°F (41°C) in July

Average Low Temperature: In Dubai, 58°F (14°C) in January, 86°F (30°C) in July

Average Annual Rainfall: 4 to 6 inches (10 to 15 cm)

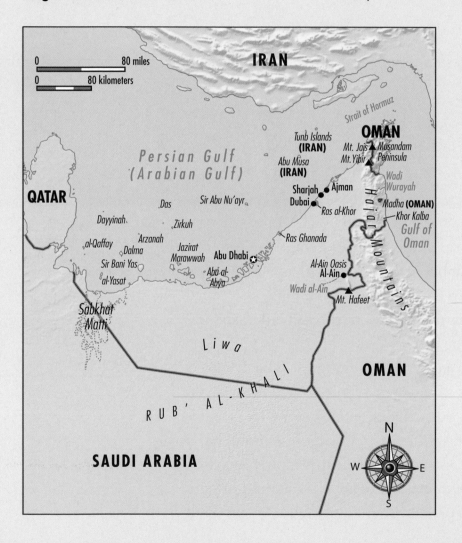

Desert and Mountain

Like the rest of the Arabian Peninsula, the United Arab Emirates is mostly desert. There are no rivers. There are no lakes. There is fresh water, but it lies deep underground. Only an occasional oasis marks the presence of water.

Along the southern border of the UAE, the desert seems overwhelming. That area is called the Rub' al-Khali, the Empty Quarter. It is the largest sand desert on Earth. While many think crossing this desert is impossible, Bedouin people have crossed the Empty Quarter for centuries, first on camels and now in trucks.

IRAN

OMAN

Ras al-Khaimah
Umm al-Quwain
Ajman
Dubai Sharjah
Fujairah

Persian Gulf (Arabian Gulf)

QATAR

Abu Dhabi

OMAN

SAUDI ARABIA

Emirates

■ Abu Dhabi		■ Ras al-Khaimah	
■ Ajman		■ Sharjah	
■ Fujairah		■ Umm al-Quwain	
■ Dubai			

Shifting Sands

Wind determines the size and shape of sand dunes. Dune patterns may look like waves in an ocean, ripples on a pond, or the flat, calm waters of a lake. The ripples can be several feet tall or as short as several inches. No dune patterns are permanent. A major windstorm can lift tons of sand and rearrange it in a new pattern in a matter of hours. The movement of sand may expose the hard, red bedrock lying under the sand, or sand may cover the land to even greater depths.

A winding road leads up Mount Yibir.

The UAE has only one mountain range, called the Hajar Mountains. *Hajar* is Arabic for "stone." The highest mountain in the UAE is Mount Yibir, which reaches 5,010 feet (1,527 meters). The mountains start in the northeast and run southeast through the UAE and into Oman. Although they are called stone mountains, the Hajar are rich in plant life, with varieties of plants changing as the elevation increases.

Wadis and Oases

Wadis are riverbeds that are usually dry but occasionally have water. Some are permanently muddy, while others collect what little rainfall there is into temporary pools. Wadis in the mountains tend to have more water in them because there is slightly more rain in the mountains than in the deserts.

Wadis in the UAE include Wadi al-Ain in Abu Dhabi and Wadi Wurayah in Fujairah. Wadi al-Ain has been a watering hole for animals and humans for centuries. A system of underground watercourses irrigates planted areas. The irrigation system, called a *falaj*, dates back at least three thousand years. Wadi Wurayah is home to hundreds of plant species, more than one hundred animal species, and a waterfall. The wadi has streams and pools surrounding rocky outcrops, and the presence of permanent fresh water attracts an assortment of animal species, including the Arabian tahr and the caracal lynx.

Wadi Wurayah lies in the northeastern part of the UAE. It was the first mountainous region in the country to be named a national park.

Salty Land

Salt flats, called *sabkha* in Arabic, are low-lying basins found along the coastline. Sabkhas are hot and dry. When the Persian Gulf floods, the heat quickly evaporates the water, leaving salty soil behind. The underlying water table is fairly close to the surface, and the water bubbles up because of the heat. New salt crystals form, producing a white, crusty layer on top of the soil. The amount of salt, the dryness of the region, and the limited soil mean that salt flats in the UAE do not support plants or animals.

Salt marshes and mud flats, on the other hand, buzz with life. The marshes are tidal areas that dot the coast. Scientists are looking for ways to use these salt marshes for agriculture. They are trying to grow *Salicornia*, a salt-loving plant that is both a grain and a vegetable. Conservationists, though, protest this use of the land, saying that these regions are essential habitat for migrating birds, native plants, and baby fish. So far, conservationists do not need to worry. The cost of growing *Salicornia* right now is higher than the fees earned from selling it.

An oasis is a region in the desert that has a water source. Historically, caravans moved from one oasis to another. Those oases grew into small towns and, eventually, cities. In the UAE, the two most famous oasis regions are Liwa, in southern Abu Dhabi on the edge of the Rub' al-Khali, and Al-Ain in eastern Abu Dhabi. In centuries past, the villages of Liwa were the last

People swim in a pond in the Liwa oasis region.

The Former Tropics

Millions of years ago, the UAE was home to the early relatives of elephants, hippopotamuses, horses, cows, and crocodiles. The land had a complex river system, and rain fell heavily. The soil supported many plants and animals. How do we know this? Rock formations in the western area of Abu Dhabi contain fossils of these animals, as well as fossils of fish, turtles, ostriches, and dozens of species that no longer exist. So, although now the area is endless miles of sand desert, it was once a tropical paradise.

On the Arabian Peninsula **23**

Most people in the UAE live along the coast, where they can sometimes escape the heat by playing in the water.

stop for travelers before they headed across the Empty Quarter. The villages had fresh water, plants for camels to eat, and date palms to provide food for both the travelers and their camels. Near the mountains, Al-Ain is a center for agriculture.

Hot and Dry

Since the UAE is desert, most people think that it never rains there. This is not true. Along the coast, it is quite humid, and even in dry regions it rains sometimes. In Abu Dhabi, February is the rainiest month, with 0.8 inches (2 centimeters) of rain. From June to October, usually no rain whatsoever falls.

Fujairah's climate is fed by the Gulf of Oman, and this region not only has rain, it can have serious floods. In 2012, heavy rain from Hatta to Ras al-Khaimah washed out roads and flooded neighborhoods. The actual amount of rain was slight, just 0.75 inches (1.9 cm), but Fujairah does not have storm

Brown Clouds

Strong winds present a problem in the UAE. The *shamal* blows nonstop through June and July. Occasionally, the shamal generates sand and dust storms. A shamal can gust up to 50 miles per hour (80 kilometers per hour), sending thick clouds of sand across the desert for days at a time. These storms make breathing outside difficult, push grit into homes, and make travel dangerous.

sewers to handle rainfall. The soil is dry and hard, and runoff collects in low-lying areas. The rain ran across the parched land rather than soaking into it, creating a sizable flood.

Cars plow through floodwaters in Abu Dhabi.

A woman shades herself from the scorching sun in Dubai.

In general, winters in the UAE are warm, spring and fall very warm, and summer sizzling. The highest recorded temperature in Dubai was 126 degrees Fahrenheit (52 degrees Celsius) in July 2002. Soaring temperatures are not unusual. In 2013, Dubai had a full week of temperatures over 122°F (50°C). The average high temperature in the region is 105°F (41°C) in July, and the average low temperature that month is 86°F (30°C).

The lowest recorded temperature in the UAE was 30°F (–1°C) at Mount Jais, in Ras al-Khaimah, in December 2004. Winters in the UAE are usually warm and short with an average high of 73°F (23°C) with overnight lows averaging 58°F (14°C). When temperatures drop to freezing in the UAE, conditions can be dangerous. Many homes are not heated because generally it is not needed, but elderly citizens especially suffer when it is extremely cold.

Looking at the UAE's Cities

Dubai, the capital of the emirate of Dubai, is the largest city in the United Arab Emirates, with a population of nearly 2.2 million. The city, located on the Persian Gulf, has become a tourist destination due to its elegant hotels, lavish shopping malls, and the tallest building in the world, Burj Khalifa. Dubai is also the home of Palm Jumeirah, a human-made group of islands in the shape of a palm tree.

With an estimated population of 1.5 million, Abu Dhabi is the second-largest city in the UAE, and the nation's capital. Sharjah (below), with a population of more than 500,000, is the nation's third-largest city, and the capital of Sharjah emirate. Sharjah is an industrial center in the northwest of the UAE. Highlights of the city include several remarkable souks, or marketplaces. These include the massive Blue Souk, the main marketplace in the city, and the Souk al-Markazi, which has a gold souk that sells only goods made of gold.

Al-Ain (above), with a population of more than 400,000, is a city in the emirate of Abu Dhabi. The name means "the spring," and Al-Ain is considered a garden city, filled with plant life fed by its *falaj* irrigation system. The water from underground has been quenching the thirst of travelers for more than a thousand years. Al-Ain Wildlife Park and Resort is a popular site for entertaining and educating children about the efforts being made to save endangered desert species.

Ajman, home to more than 200,000 is the largest city in the smallest emirate, also named Ajman. Ajman is known for beautiful beaches, and many visitors enjoy a trip to the dhow-building yard. Dhows are traditional wooden boats built using hand tools. An important archaeological site there is the Mowaihat tomb. Many important artifacts have been unearthed from this circular tomb, including painted ceramic pots, beads, copper tools, and the remains of the tomb's first residents.

CHAPTER 3

The Natural World

ANEWBORN TAHR HAS BEEN DISCOVERED ON Mount Hafeet in Abu Dhabi. The Environment Agency–Abu Dhabi set up motion-sensitive cameras in areas where there were hints that tahrs could be found. A mother and kid set off the motion sensors, and scientists could not be happier. The photo of a newborn answers the question of whether the UAE could support the restoration of tahrs in the Hajar Mountains. Arabian tahrs are mountain goats that are among the rarest mammals in the UAE. During the twentieth century, the number of tahrs dwindled because of hunting. It is not easy to protect tahrs because they are rarely seen. In recent years, however, several female tahrs with kids have been seen in Fujairah's Wadi Wurayah area. It will be some time before the tahr population is secure, but every birth is progress.

Opposite: **Both male and female tahrs have long, arching horns.**

Necessary Adaptations

Many UAE ecosystems are extreme. The desert is dry, hot, and sandy. Mangrove trees thrive in coastal wetlands, even in the very salty water of the Gulf of Oman. Species that require large amounts of fresh water make the sharp, rocky Hajar Mountains their home. In the mountains, they drink from pools in the wadis that lie between peaks.

Plants and animals have adapted to their harsh environment in order to survive. Antelopes called oryx live in the deepest desert and never drink water. They take in water only by eating plants. Other species that live in the UAE sleep through the day and feed or move only at night. Snakes usually

Flamingos feed near the mangroves at Ras al-Khor Wildlife Sanctuary in Dubai. Sometimes, more than three thousand flamingos settle at Ras al-Khor in the winter.

Arabian Oryx

The Arabian oryx once freely roamed the deserts of what is now the United Arab Emirates. By the early 1960s, the oryx was nearly extinct. Oryx are the largest members of the antelope family, and they have two long curved horns. For years, hunters killed Arabian oryx so they could mount the antlers on their walls. The last wild Arabian oryx was killed in 1972. By that time, there was already a breeding program on Sir Bani Yas Island, off the coast of Abu Dhabi. The program began with three female and two male oryx. Over time, breeding programs at Sir Bani Yas, Al-Ain Wildlife Park, and other preserves have produced healthy herds of oryx. Between 2007 and 2012, five hundred oryx were reintroduced into the deep desert near Liwa.

thrive in the daylight when the sun's rays warm their bodies. Yet, in the UAE, the horned viper is almost exclusively nocturnal. The Arabian toad and the Dhofar toad overcome the extreme dryness in a unique way. They can burrow deep into the mud of a wadi and lie dormant for three years or more. Plants have adapted by sending long taproots into the earth to obtain water. The ghaf's taproot can reach as deep as 115 feet (35 m) into the soil in search of water.

Among the Desert Sands

The desert sand dunes of the United Arab Emirates support many plants, and those plants, in turn, provide food for many animals. Beneath the yellow blossoms of the Arabian primrose, a brown-and-beige Arabian sand boa blends in with its

The Arabian toad-headed agama raises and curls its tail to attract a mate.

surroundings. The sand boa feeds mainly on desert geckos and worm lizards. The Arabian sand gecko has webbed feet, which are helpful for walking on soft sand. Geckos are burrow dwellers, as are Arabian toad-headed agamas, awl-headed snakes, and several species of sandfish. Common sandfish move under the sand, rather than on it, which helps them avoid predators.

Ghaf: The National Tree

The ghaf provides welcome shade from the desert heat of the UAE. A tall evergreen tree, ghafs can reach up to 82 feet (25 m) tall. The trees produce tiny flowers on spikes from March to May and again from October to January. Ghafs also produce cylinder-shaped, reddish-brown seedpods. In Al-Ain, the local government called on its citizens to help with pruning the ghaf trees lining city streets. Pruning ghafs is a skill passed from father to son, and the city needs skilled people to tend these trees.

Tamarisk and *Prosopis* trees provide welcome shade for desert-dwelling creatures. Prickly lettuce, purslane, astragalus, and senna are among the many low-lying plants that provide animals with food, shelter, and nesting material. Several bird species, including desert larks and bar-tailed larks, feed on seeds from desert plants. Bar-tailed larks burrow with plant-eating lizards during the hottest times of day. Various species of cleome provide brightly colored flowers for nectar-loving bees and butterflies living on the dunes. Even grasshoppers find sufficient grasses to make the desert their home.

Several types of cleome flowers thrive in the United Arab Emirates.

The National Flower

The UAE's national flower is the *tribulus omanense*, or puncture vine, a desert shrub with bright yellow flowers. The shrub thrives even in the driest desert thanks to its extremely long taproot, which also anchors the plant on open dunes, shifting sands, or gravel plains. The plant's flowers feature five oval petals and a sweet nectar.

Honey badgers are fierce predators with powerful jaws. They hunt snakes, turtles, birds, rodents, and any other creatures they can find.

The largest animals in the desert are goitered gazelles, oryx, honey badgers, jackals, and Rüppel's foxes. The goitered gazelles are herbivores, feeding on a wide variety of grasses and shrubs. Jackals and foxes are carnivores, which

have to compete with birds of prey, such as the Brahminy kite and the Eurasian griffon. These predators tend to live on the edges of the desert or near seeps that provide needed water. Desert predators feed on whatever they can find. Golden jackals, for example, feed on birds and rodents, bird eggs, large insects, and carrion, or dead animals. Jackals live in breeding pairs and build dens underground or in abandoned termite hills.

The warmth of the desert makes it a welcome home for snakes and lizards. In addition to sand boas, the UAE's deserts are home to several species of vipers, hooked-thread snakes, and Schokari sand racers—the fastest moving snakes on the Arabian Peninsula.

Many insects survive in the desert. African babul blue butterflies, fat-tailed scorpions, dull brown desert mantises, and desert runner ants thrive in the intense heat and dryness of the desert. Black pennant dragonflies can live almost anywhere. They lay their eggs in and near water, but there are many black pennant adults found in the desert.

Creepy Crawlers

Scorpions are among the nastiest creatures in the UAE. They deliver bites that can send a human to the hospital, or even kill a person. Scorpions try to avoid humans, but they do crawl into tents, under rocks, and into shoes. It is a good idea when camping in the UAE to shake out all shoes and clothes before getting dressed to make sure there are no scorpions hiding. Scorpions generally live two to five years, but the UAE has one species that can live up to twenty-five years. Fourteen species of scorpions live everywhere in the UAE from the desert to the Hajar Mountains.

In the Mountains

The Hajar Mountains have all the essentials for a thriving ecosystem: food, water, and shelter. From a distance, there seems to be little difference between the mountains and the desert. They both seem bleak. A close-up view finds a full range of grasses, shrubs, wildflowers, and trees. All life centers on the wadis and seeps, where water is available.

Species in Danger: Arabian Leopard

Arabian leopards are native to the UAE but are extremely rare. They are the largest cats in the region but the smallest of the world's leopard species. The Arabian leopard has been brought to the brink of extinction as a result of loss of habitat, limited range, and overhunting. There are only about two hundred Arabian leopards in existence worldwide.

Clusters of annual rabbit-foot grass, bishop's weed, and desert cotton provide excellent hiding places for ground birds, such as the sand partridge, sand grouse, and the chukar. Chukars feed mainly on seeds, but partridges and grouse prefer a broader diet of seeds and insects. Although they have plenty of food and shelter, these ground birds had best be wary. Golden jackals and Arabian leopards put ground birds, their eggs, and their hatchlings high on their choice of prey.

The wadis also attract insects, including the brilliant red scarlet darters, blue-green elegant sprites, and Hajar wadi

Chukars thrive in dry areas so long as they can find water to drink. They get their name from the "chuk chuk" call of the males.

Girls Only

The Brahminy blind snake is a small wormlike snake that lives in agricultural areas of the UAE and many other places around the world. It has the distinction of being one of the few unisexual snakes on Earth. No males have ever been found, yet the females are able to produce young. The Brahminy blind snake lives underground and feeds on ants, termites, and insect larvae.

damsels. These species need water to reproduce. Their larvae live in the wadis, while the parents buzz around desert cotton and bright pink wild geraniums. Darters, sprites, and damselflies make excellent eating for lizards, toads, and songbirds. The shrubs and thickets are alive with song from a variety of sparrows, warblers, and buntings.

The black-headed bunting is noted for its bright yellow stomach and black head.

Many mountain creatures have distinct coloration that allows them to hide in plain sight. The gray-brown coloring of the death's head hawkmoth enables the moth to camp unseen on the branches of Christ's thorn and olive trees. But probably the best-camouflaged species in the Hajars is the scops owl. Its mixture of gray and brown feathering allows it to be nearly invisible perched on a tree limb.

The mountains host a range of birds of prey that feast on a wide variety of species. The peregrine falcon prefers songbirds, which it captures in flight. The saker falcon, on the other hand, is a ferocious hunter and will take on much larger animals. Easy hunting brings the saker small rodents and songbirds, but it will also hunt hares and owls. Pharaoh eagle-owls roost on mountain cliffs and prefer a diet of snakes, lizards, beetles, and scorpions.

The Cycle of Life

In the arid Hajar Mountains, every plant is an important part of the ecosystem. For example, the wild oat and wild wheat plants offer nesting material and food for the partridges and grouse. The seeds are ideal for hooded wheatear birds and Libyan jirds, a type of rodent. Grasshoppers gnaw these plants down to the roots. Butterflies take nectar when the oats and wheat are in flower. All these insects draw lizards and insect-eating birds. Snakes hide in the grasses, ready to pounce when gerbils and jerboas come to feed. Pharaoh eagle-owls (right) keep a sharp eye on the shrubs, hunting for the snakes and lizards that will make up their next meals. Mountain gazelles and tahrs consider wild oats and wild wheat a feast, and Arabian leopards, though rare, devour gazelles and tahrs.

Salt Marshes and Mangrove Swamps

Emirati salt marshes have high salt content, but the water is loaded with fish, which draws wading birds and waterbirds in large numbers. Black-and-white avocets and common cranes are among the wading birds dipping their bills for a treat. The garganey and the ruddy shelduck, two rather unusual relatives of the duck, have coloring that blends in with brown and gray reeds. When not feeding, they hide among the reeds.

Mangroves are unusual trees in that they grow directly in salt water, which will kill most plants. Mangrove swamps are important habitats on coastlines around the world. They form a unique marine ecosystem. The forests serve as breeding sites for three-fourths of the sea snakes, sea turtles, shrimp, and fish such as snapper, grouper, and grunt. Mangrove trees are short, growing only 10 to 16 feet (3 to 5 m) tall.

The UAE's mangrove swamps lie along the east coast in Fujairah and to the west in Abu Dhabi. Khor Kalba is the most northerly mangrove forest in the world.

Migrating birds use Khor Kalba as a rest stop on their journeys between Asia and Africa. In mangrove swamps, tiny bar-tailed godwits use their long, thin beaks to poke in the mud to reach tasty critters. Black storks and Indian pond herons are among the long-legged birds that wade through the waters in search of small fish, while several different species of terns soar overhead. Branches of mangrove trees provide

About three-quarters of all the mangrove trees in the UAE are in Abu Dhabi. Mangrove forests help protect the coastline from erosion caused by the waves.

roosting for thrush nightingales, Sykes's warblers, and forest wagtails. By far the most colorful visitor is the Alexandrine parakeet, sporting brilliant green feathers, a yellow-tipped bill, and a pinkish circle around its neck.

Human interference is destroying mangrove habitats. Litter, particularly plastic bags, creates an unsightly mess. It also endangers the birds, fish, and marine mammals living in the waters. The UAE participates in International Mangrove Day by planting thousands of saplings and running programs to educate visitors about the dangers of polluting the mangrove habitat.

Tourists kayak through the wetlands on Sir Bani Yas Island, a wildlife reserve off the coast of Abu Dhabi.

In Coastal Waters

Coastal islands provide nesting for hawksbill sea turtles, and nurseries for everything from the clubnose guitarfish to jarbua terapons and annulated sea snakes. Just off the coast, the UAE has extensive coral reefs that feature dozens of coral species. Coral comes in many shapes, sizes, and colors. Some look like brains. Others look like fans, ferns, lettuce, or honeycomb.

The UAE's coral reefs are complete ecosystems unto themselves. Healthy coral reefs attract tropical fish. The water is warm and clear, and angelfish, clown fish, and butterfly fish swim around the coral reef ecosystem. Small fish attract midsize fish, such as five-lined snapper, wrasse, and grouper. These midsize fish attract the larger rays and sharks.

Fish swim by the brilliantly colored coral reef near Dubai.

A desalination plant in Dubai. Desalination plants supply 99 percent of the fresh water in Dubai. Only 1 percent comes from groundwater.

Conservation and the Environment

The UAE faces a number of challenges in its efforts to protect the environment. One of the greatest problems is water. There is no more water available in the UAE today than there was one hundred years ago, but the population has increased dramatically. The government works hard to meet the need for water through desalination plants, which remove the salt from seawater to make it drinkable. The plants produce 2.2 billion cubic yards (1.7 billion cubic meters) of fresh water every year. This water allows cities such as Dubai and Abu Dhabi to support parks and public gardens.

Desert climates do not encourage the growth of trees. The government protects ghaf trees, but for some tree species, environmental awareness came too late. The *Rhizophora mucronata* species, a type of flowering mangrove, disappeared from the UAE about one hundred years ago. Pakistan provided the UAE with seeds for this particular mangrove, and a mangrove nursery was created at Ras Ghanada Island. The species has been restored, and the new mangrove plantation is one of the largest in the UAE.

What Ras Ghanada Island is to mangroves, Sir Bani Yas is to oryx, houbara bustards, Somali ostriches, caracals, striped hyenas, and northern cheetahs. Sir Bani Yas was a vacation home for UAE president Sheikh Zayed bin Sultan al-Nahyan. In the early 1970s, the sheikh began bringing endangered animals to the island. The island was turned into a wildlife reserve in 1977, and it soon became an important breeding site for regional endangered species. The greatest success of Sir Bani Yas's conservation efforts is the oryx. A breeding plan for oryx produced a large herd that now roams freely on the island.

A herd of thirty-seven giraffes lives on Sir Bani Yas.

CHAPTER 4

Young Nation, Long History

THE UNITED ARAB EMIRATES HAS ONLY BEEN IN existence since 1971, but that does not mean Emiratis do not have a long heritage. The history of the Arabian Peninsula stretches back 7,500 years. As early as 5500 BCE, Abu Dhabi and Sharjah had become centers for harvesting pearls.

Opposite: **For centuries, merchants used camels to transport trade goods across the dry lands of Arabia.**

Across the Desert

Around 2000 BCE, camels were domesticated in Arabia. Before humans raised and trained camels, there was no way to cross the desert. Traveling by camel gave merchants an alternative to traveling by the sea. The only problem was that water was scarce. The discovery of oases at Liwa and Al-Ain provided a solution. Camel caravans soon crisscrossed the desert, stopping at Al-Ain, which became a trade hub.

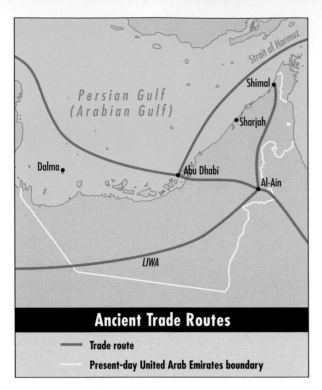

Ancient Trade Routes

— Trade route

— Present-day United Arab Emirates boundary

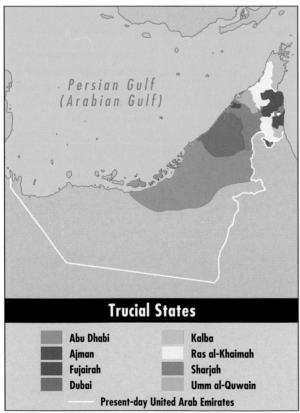

Trucial States

Abu Dhabi
Ajman
Fujairah
Dubai
Kalba
Ras al-Khaimah
Sharjah
Umm al-Quwain

— Present-day United Arab Emirates

In the seventh century CE, the Umayyad dynasty took control of the region that is now the United Arab Emirates. The Umayyads were the first major Muslim dynasty. Although the family was based in Mecca, in what is now Saudi Arabia, the dynasty ruled Damascus, Syria. The Umayyads introduced the Bedouin people of what is now the UAE to the Arabic language and the Muslim religion.

The Trucial States

By the 1800s, the British were trading in the Persian Gulf and the Gulf of Oman. Qasimi people sailed the same seas and sometimes attacked the ships that passed their territory, taking their goods. The British called them pirates. The British responded to the Qasimi attacks by destroying the ports of Ras al-Khaimah and other Arab seaports. The British ended the violence at sea by insisting on a truce in 1820.

At the time, the region consisted of a loose connection of sheikhdoms. They became known as the Trucial States, after the truces the sheikhdoms signed

Al Fahidi Fort in Dubai was built around 1787 to protect the sheikhdom there from attacks by neighboring groups. It is the oldest standing building in Dubai.

with the British. Abu Dhabi, Dubai, Ras al-Khaimah, Ajman, Umm al-Quwain, Fujairah, and Sharjah were independent in some regards but under British rule in others. In 1892, another agreement was signed giving the British the responsibility for military defense and foreign relations.

Life in the Trucial States was much as it had always been for the residents. In the summer, people flocked to the coast to work in the pearling industry. In the winter months, they harvested and processed dates from date palms. The seaports grew into cities, but many citizens continued a somewhat nomadic existence moving between the coast and inland date oases.

Pearl divers would swim to the bottom of the sea to collect oysters that might contain pearls. Sailors in boats would help pull the divers back to the surface.

Troubled Times

From 1914 through 1918, World War I raged in Europe. Abu Dhabi and other coastal areas still thrived on the pearling industry. As the war continued, however, selling pearls became less profitable. When the Great Depression began in 1929, the world economy struggled, and there was no market for pearls. Then, in the early 1930s, Japan developed cultured pearls, and the pearling industry was doomed.

Oil was discovered on the Arabian Peninsula in 1931, but not in the Trucial States. At the time, the world still suffered from an economic depression, and money for exploration was tight. The British still held control in the region, but British rule was stretched thin. Exploring for oil on the Arabian Peninsula required a lot of money, and there were too many pressing issues in the rest of the British Empire to allow for exploration.

By the end of the 1930s, the British were engaged in World War II. While the British were busy elsewhere, trouble erupted between Dubai and its neighbor Sharjah. Minor arguments exploded into armed conflict, and the British brought about a quick end to the dispute by cutting off aid to both sides. The minor battles ended, mainly because both sides ran out of gunpowder and other goods.

World War II affected the Trucial States because the war cut off seagoing trade. The lack of trade and the end of pearling left people on the coast in poverty. Recovery and change would come, but not until the war ended.

In the middle of the twentieth century, Dubai was still a small city with a population of less than fifty thousand.

Oil!

The fortune of the emirates was about to change. Oil exploration during the late 1950s and early 1960s proved productive. Oil was discovered in Abu Dhabi in 1958, and exports began in 1962. The first wells in Dubai struck oil in 1966 from the offshore Fateh field. More exploration discovered more opportunities for successful drilling. It turned out that the UAE owns about 10 percent of the world's crude oil supply.

The sale of oil made Abu Dhabi wealthy, but it did nothing for everyday people. Sheikh Shakhbut, who had ruled Abu Dhabi since 1928, held onto the money. He was forced to give up his position in 1966. His brother Sheikh Zayed bin Sultan al-Nahyan took over as the new ruler.

Several vast oil fields have been discovered in the remote deserts of Abu Dhabi.

Founding the UAE

By this time, the United Kingdom had lost interest in continuing to administer the Trucial States. It was simply too expensive. In 1971, the United Arab Emirates became independent. There was much to do. The new country needed currency, which had to be designed, printed, and ready for distribution. It needed a postal system, a banking system, a flag, and a system of organizing the government. The government's basic foundation would be determined by a constitution, and that document had to be written and agreed upon by all members of the UAE. The UAE also needed a budget, a way to fund the budget, and a ruling body that would deal with the economy, foreign relations, and domestic issues.

Sheikh Shakhbut (center) was forced from power by his younger brother, Sheikh Zayed bin Sultan al-Nahyan. He lived in exile in England for several years before being allowed to return to Abu Dhabi.

The First President

In 1971, Sheikh Zayed bin Sultan al-Nahyan (1918–2004) became the UAE's first president, an office he held for thirty-three years. Zayed had been raised in Al-Ain and lived for some time in the desert with Bedouin people. In 1946, he was appointed the governor of the Eastern Region of Abu Dhabi, mainly the area around Al-Ain, and then became the emir of Abu Dhabi in 1966. In the years after, he helped organize the United Arab Emirates and got the emirates to work together. As president of the UAE, he used wealth the country acquired from the oil industry to help raise the standard of living for all Emiratis. He remained president until his death in 2004.

The UAE chose Sheikh Zayed bin Sultan al-Nahyan, emir of Abu Dhabi, as its first president in 1971. Sheikh Zayed was a visionary leader who saw that the UAE's newfound oil wealth could raise the standard of living of all UAE citizens. He introduced extensive housing projects, education reform, the building of transportation routes, and development of a nationwide health care system.

Historically, the emirs ruled their lands as the first among equals. They had advisers, but the people had no say in what happened. They were, however, regularly overthrown when the people were not satisfied with their rule. When Sheikh Zayed died in 2004, his son Sheikh Khalifa inherited the job.

In 2006, the UAE tested the idea of an elected government by establishing the Federal National Council. This body had both appointed and elected officials. The first vote was by an electoral college of fewer than 7,000 citizens. It was an experiment. Today, there is still an electoral college, but it has more than 125,000 voters, 46 percent of whom are women.

In 2008, a global financial crisis struck and affected the UAE in several ways. Construction halted on major building projects in Dubai. Real estate values dropped by half. Many people who worked in construction and finance lost their jobs.

In Dubai, many construction sites were abandoned, leaving skyscrapers unfinished, during the financial crisis that began in 2008.

Loss of money has not been the only issue to plague the UAE in recent years. The emirs have had to contend with the effects of modern communications as well. The rise of the Internet and cell phones led people to exercise freedom of speech. Criticism of the government led to rebellion as the government tried to tighten its grip on antigovernment political comments. Groups in favor of democracy, such as Al-Islah, circulated an online petition to end leadership by

Computers and cell phones are common in the UAE, making it harder for the government to limit people's speech.

the emirs and start an elected government. In 2012, the emirs made criticizing the government either in public or via the Internet against the law. Pro-democracy groups continue to protest, and many people who disagree with the emirs have been sentenced to jail.

Many Emiratis, including this blogger who was later pardoned, have been jailed for criticizing the government.

Masdar: An Alternative to Oil

In 2005, the UAE became the first major oil producer to sign the Kyoto Protocol, an international agreement to find energy alternatives to fossil fuels such as oil and coal. Abu Dhabi has invested more than $20 billion in an alternative energy program called Masdar. Masdar City is a totally "green" city. All facilities and housing there rely on solar power. Ultimately, the city will house around 50,000 people and support 1,500 businesses.

CHAPTER 5

Ruling the Emirates

THE UNITED ARAB EMIRATES IS A FEDERATION OF seven emirates that govern jointly and support a strong economic platform. Although the emirates are tied to one another, they are more independent than U.S. states. The emirs govern their own territories and territorial waters. The United Arab Emirates was formed in 1971, with a constitution declaring the rights and responsibilities of the emirs and the people of the UAE.

The Constitution

The constitution declares that the UAE is part of a greater Arab nation, and all Arab citizens are tied together by religion, language, and tradition. Islam is the official religion of the UAE, and Arabic is the official language. The constitution names the city of Abu Dhabi as the capital. Trade and travel among the emirates are open, with no tolls, taxes, or restrictions for Emirati citizens.

Elderly men relax in Dubai.

The constitution also declares that the family is the corner-stone of the community. The community bears the responsibility of caring for children and mothers. The UAE assists citizens who are elderly, sick, or incapable of caring for themselves.

The National Flag

The United Arab Emirates flag was adopted in 1971, when the United Arab Emirates became one nation. When the UAE was first considered, a competition was held to design a flag. The flag chosen was designed by Abdulla Mohammed al-Ma'enah. It features green, white, black, and red, which represent the unity of the seven emirates. The four colors symbolize parts of a poem by Safi al-Din al-Hilli. In the poem, the motives of the Arab fighters were pure (white), but the battles were fierce (black). The lands were lush (green), yet the Arab swords were stained with blood (red).

The government recognizes specific rights of citizens. This includes the concept that all citizens are equal under the law, with no bias according to race, religion, or social status. UAE citizens have rights similar to those of U.S. citizens. For example, citizens cannot be held or put in jail without a trial and conviction. Punishments for crimes are set by law, and people must be proven guilty in a fair trial. People may choose their work, religion, and beliefs. Freedom of speech is guaranteed unless that speech is against the law.

A court building in Dubai

Finally, the constitution establishes a federal government. This government consists of the Federal Supreme Council, the UAE president and vice president, a federal Council of Ministers, the Federal National Council, and a federal judiciary.

The UAE Executive

The Federal Supreme Council is at the top of the executive branch of the United Arab Emirates. It has seven members—the rulers of each emirate. The council deals with major issues such as defense, foreign policy, and maintaining the economic health of the nation.

Sheikh Mohammed bin Rashid al-Maktoum, the vice president of the UAE and ruler of Dubai, speaks before the Federal National Council.

The council also selects the president and vice president from among its own members. The president is the official head of state. The first president was Sheikh Zayed bin Sultan al-Nahyan. He held office from 1971 until his death in 2004, when his son, Sheikh Khalifa bin Zayed al-Nahyan became the new president. So far, the president has always been from Abu Dhabi, the largest and wealthiest of the emirates. The current vice president is Sheikh Mohammed bin Rashid al-Maktoum of Dubai, who also serves as prime minister. Dubai, the second-largest and second-wealthiest emirate, has provided all but one vice president and every prime minister.

Emiratis vote for candidates for the Federal National Council.

The Council of Ministers is a cabinet that advises the Federal Supreme Council. Ministers offer advice in specific areas that affect the UAE. The ministries include foreign affairs, justice, public health, finance and economy, education, and agriculture. Most members of the Council of Ministers are relatives of the current emirs.

The Head of Government

Sheikh Mohammed bin Rashid al-Maktoum (1949–) is the ruler of Dubai, the UAE's vice president, and the prime minister of the government. Sheikh Mohammed is a reformer and motivator. He is credited with Dubai's growth as a global center for business and finance. He assisted in launching Emirates Airline, DP World (a company that owns ports around the world), and the Jumeirah Group (a hotel chain), which he owns through a holding company called Dubai Holding. He also founded the Mohammed Bin Rashid School of Government.

In 2004, Sheikha Lubna bint Khalid bin Sultan al-Qasimi (1962–) became the first female minister in the UAE government when she became the minister for foreign trade. She is a member of Sharjah's al-Qasimi family. Sheikha Lubna received a degree in computer science from California State University, Chico, before earning a graduate degree in business from the University of Sharjah. As part of the UAE government, she has led efforts to contribute more money to help other nations. In fact, in 2013, the UAE donated US$5.4 billion to other nations, a total of 1.3 percent of its national income. That's a higher percentage than any other country has donated. Because of these efforts, Sheikha Lubna is considered one of the most powerful women in the world.

Federal National Council

The UAE's Federal National Council is an advisory body. It does not have the power to pass any laws, but rather can only recommend changes in laws and policies. It has forty members, and seats are determined according to the population in each emirate. Half of the members are elected, and half are appointed. The members serve four-year terms. In the current Federal National Council, eight members are women.

The Judicial System

The UAE has a federal court system. While the emirates usually come together in most aspects of ruling the region, this is not true in the legal system. Dubai and Ras al-Khaimah each

The National Government of the United Arab Emirates

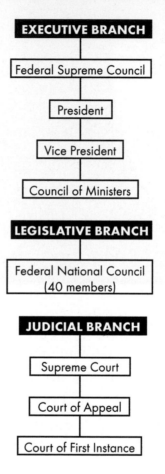

EXECUTIVE BRANCH

Federal Supreme Council

President

Vice President

Council of Ministers

LEGISLATIVE BRANCH

Federal National Council
(40 members)

JUDICIAL BRANCH

Supreme Court

Court of Appeal

Court of First Instance

have their own court systems and do not participate in the UAE federal courts.

The highest court in the UAE federal court system is the Supreme Court, which is located in Abu Dhabi. Cases are heard in the Court of First Instance. These cases can be reviewed by a Court of Appeal.

The National Anthem

The national anthem of the UAE is "Ishy Bilady," which means "Long Live My Nation." The melody was composed by Mohammed Abdel Wahab and adopted in 1971 after the UAE had been formed. The lyrics, written by Arif al-Sheikh Abdullah al-Hassan, became official twenty-five years later, in 1996.

English translation

Live, my country, the unity of our Emirates.

You have lived for a nation.

Whose religion is Islam, and whose guide is the Qur'an.

I made you stronger in the name of God, O homeland.

My country, my country, my country, my country.

May God protect you from the evil through time.

We have vowed to build and work.

Work sincerely, work sincerely.

As long as we live we'll be sincere, sincere.

May safety last, and the flag rise, O Emirates.

The symbol of Arabness.

We all make sacrifices for you, we supply you with our blood.

A traditional majlis in Abu Dhabi. Both the room and the meeting are called a majlis.

Local Governments

Local governments handle the everyday workings of cities and towns. Each emirate has its own executive council, run mainly by the emir and members of the emir's family. Emirates have established agencies to promote business and tourism at home. Abu Dhabi, Ajman, Dubai, and Sharjah have environmental departments, tourism councils, and health authorities.

It is a tradition that emirs hold open discussions with the people of their emirate, similar to town hall meetings. When an emir holds an open *majlis* (consultation), merchants, nobles, and commoners are free to present ideas or problems to the rulers. On occasion, a ruling emir might appoint family members to hear the concerns of the local people. This tradition is important to the Emiratis, and all people are heard and their concerns weighed seriously.

Abu Dhabi: The Capital City

A city of stunning monuments, wide boulevards, and unique modern architecture, Abu Dhabi, the capital of the UAE, is considered the Arabian jewel. The city is located on an island that is connected to the mainland by a bridge. It is a relatively young city. It was first settled in 1761, and by 1900 it had only about six thousand residents. Today, the city is growing quickly, with a population of about 1.5 million.

To get a better view of Abu Dhabi, people take the elevator at Etihad Towers to the observation deck. From there, visitors can scan the cityscape, with its blend of old and new architecture. Among the most beautiful sights in Abu Dhabi is the Sheikh Zayed Grand Mosque. The

mosque features artistic glasswork, mosaic tiles, and intricate carvings throughout the building. After a trip to the mosque, visitors head for the al-Hosn Palace, also called the Old Fort or the White Fort. It is Abu Dhabi's oldest building. The courtyard is stunning, with incredible tile work. Unique to Abu Dhabi is the Falcon Hospital, the only one in the world. For anyone who has ever wanted to hold a falcon, this is the place to go. Finally, no trip to Abu Dhabi would be complete without visiting the souks. *Souk* means market, and today's souks sell everything from fresh vegetables and fruits to freshly caught fish to carpets and mattresses. The most traditional souk is Souk al-Zafarana, which offers incense, spices, Arab clothing, musical instruments, coffee pots, and a host of other truly Emirati goods.

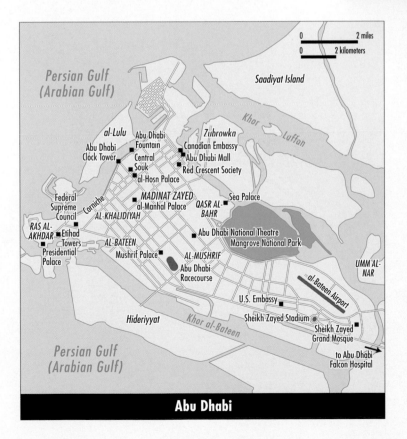

Abu Dhabi

CHAPTER 6

Wealth From Oil

UNTIL RECENTLY, THE UAE ECONOMY DEPENDED heavily on petroleum, or oil. Although the UAE approaches the world market as a country, each emirate runs its own economy, and each emirate attracts investments in different ways. Some provide tax-free work environments, while others provide extensive research facilities or land for building manufacturing plants.

Getting Past Petroleum

The UAE government knows that dependence on oil could harm the economy in the long run. Its first priority is to get more Emirati people to work. The emirs want to bring in more manufacturing, increase agricultural efforts, and expand trade relationships.

Currently, foreign workers make up 80 percent of the country's population but 95 percent of its workers. The government leaders hope to change the profile of the workforce so that 20 percent of workers will be native Emiratis. To accomplish this, the UAE has funded sixteen technical colleges that teach information technology, applied technology, and dozens of labor-specific courses.

Manufacturing

Manufacturing and other industries make up about 59 percent of the country's gross domestic product, the total value of all goods and services produced in the country. The Ministry of Economy estimates that the country has more than five

A man moves colorful textiles at a market in Dubai.

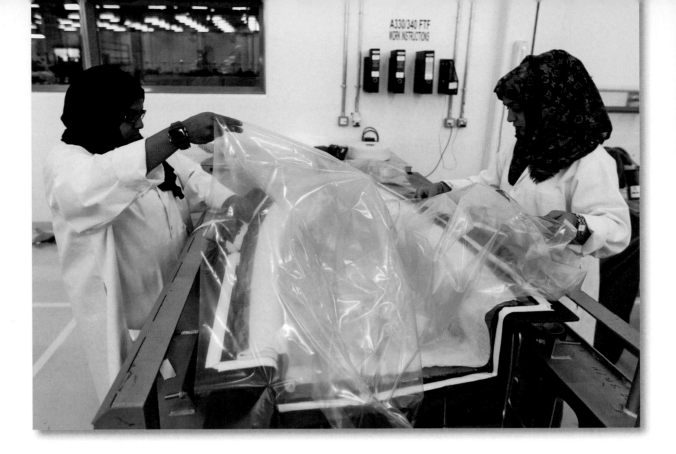

thousand industrial companies. The main industries are food and beverages, chemicals, mineral products, paper products, textiles, clothing, and wood products. Firms also turn out aluminum, chemicals, steel, and marine industry products. Polyolefin, a material used to make foam, insulation, and other products, is a major manufactured good. Three-fourths of the country's manufactured exports go to Asian countries.

Four out of ten manufacturing firms are located in Dubai, and Sharjah has another 30 percent. But investment will soon change the manufacturing profile of the county. Sixty percent of investments in manufacturing in recent years have been in Abu Dhabi, and just over 20 percent of investments have been in Dubai.

Women work at a factory in Al-Ain that manufactures airplane parts.

What the UAE Grows, Makes, and Mines

AGRICULTURE

Dates	725,000 metric tons
Poultry	43,000 metric tons
Tomatoes	62.7 metric tons

MANUFACTURING

Cement	15,000,000 metric tons
Aluminum	890,000 metric tons
Steel products	90,000 metric tons

MINING

Oil	2.8 million barrels per day
Natural gas	54 million cubic meters per day
Quarried stone	100 metric tons

Agriculture

Agriculture is a very small part of the UAE economy. It accounts for less than 1 percent of all the goods and services produced there.

The UAE is heavily invested in getting the most from its farms and providing as much as possible of the food its population needs. The barriers to successful farming are great. The majority of the land is not suitable for farming. The climate is hot and water is scarce.

The most important crop in the UAE is dates. The emirates currently have 16 million date palm trees that produce more than 800,000 tons (725,000 metric tons) of dates every year. That is 11 percent of all dates grown worldwide.

The government sponsors a number of research facilities to promote agriculture. Test farms, computer-run greenhouses, and innovations in irrigation have helped farmers produce larger crops each year. In addition, farmers get money back from the government for purchases of farm machinery, seed, fertilizers, and other farm goods. Though government assistance has more than tripled the number of farms in ten years, only 7 percent

Dates are piled high at a market in Sharjah. About 160 different varieties of dates are grown in the UAE.

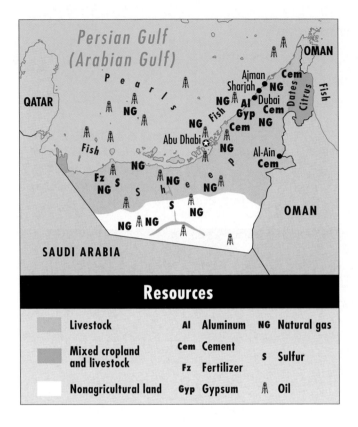

Persian Gulf (Arabian Gulf)

QATAR

Pearls

Fish

SAUDI ARABIA

Abu Dhabi

Ajman
Sharjah
Dubai
Al-Ain

OMAN

OMAN

Dates
Citrus
Fish

Resources

▨ Livestock	**Al** Aluminum	**NG** Natural gas
▨ Mixed cropland and livestock	**Cem** Cement	**s** Sulfur
▨ Nonagricultural land	**Fz** Fertilizer	
	Gyp Gypsum	⚒ Oil

of workers are involved in agriculture. Ras al-Khaimah has the most farms, mainly because runoff water from the Hajar Mountains provides adequate water for growing crops. And other emirates are growing more produce than ever before. In 2014, the Abu Dhabi Farmers Services Centre reported that local farmers had grown 11,000 tons (10,000 metric tons) more vegetables than in the previous year.

Besides dates, the UAE also grows melons, citrus, and mangoes. Major vegetable products grown in the UAE are tomatoes, cabbage, eggplant, squash, and cauliflower. Poultry farming meets 70 percent of the consumer demand for eggs and about half the need for poultry meat. Dairy farms produce about 90 percent of the milk and milk products used in the UAE.

Fishing is a major source of protein for UAE residents, but fisheries have been greatly overfished. The government offers financial help for fishers to buy boats and equipment. In addition, the government has active programs to promote aquaculture. The Marine Environmental Research Center supplements Persian Gulf fishing stocks. In the 2012–2013 season, 2.8 million young fish were released into UAE waters. Common species include grouper, mackeral, tuna, mullet, and sea bream.

Oil and Gas

The United Arab Emirates is the world's sixth-largest producer of petroleum and petroleum products. The nation produces 2.8 million barrels of crude oil a day. Gas producers pump 54 million cubic meters of gas per day. At the current rate of use, UAE petroleum reserves should last 100 to 125 years.

A number of spin-offs from oil and gas production have expanded the UAE's economic outlook. Petroleum processing in Abu Dhabi has grown from 485,000 barrels per day to 885,000 barrels per day. The UAE manufactures a wide variety of chemical products, including fertilizers and pesticides. The plastics industry, another offshoot of petroleum, is growing by double-digit percentages each year. A stinky but profitable by-product of the gas industry is sulfur. Extracted from sour gas, sulfur from Abu Dhabi is used to make fertilizers, rubber, and sulfuric acid.

A fish market in Sharjah. About 75,000 metric tons of fish are caught and sold in the UAE every year.

About 4.5 million foreign workers live in the United Arab Emirates. Most people employed in the construction industry in the UAE are foreign workers.

Importing and Exporting

In 2014, the UAE imported about $272 billion in goods, and that number is rising each year. The major imports include machinery and transportation equipment, chemicals, and food. The main suppliers of these goods are China, India, the United States, and Germany.

Exports go mainly to Asian nations, with the main destinations being Japan, India, Iran, South Korea, and Thailand. The largest export is crude oil, which accounts for 45 percent of exported goods. The UAE also exports natural gas, dried fish, and dates. The annual value of exports is about $400 billion.

There is one other commodity the UAE imports, and that is labor. The majority of the country's labor force comes from South Asian countries, including Pakistan, India, and Thailand. Many workers also come from Iran, Syria, and Yemen. Most foreign workers are employed in construction, oil and gas industries, or service industries.

Service Sector

In service industries, workers do things for other people rather than making, growing, or mining products. In the UAE, services make up about 40 percent of the economy. Major service industries include banking, education, health care, sales, and tourism. Despite the heat and the desert, the UAE is fast becoming a tourist destination. Dubai is the entertainment hub of the Middle East. In addition to its beaches and warm-water seas, the UAE is home to popular theme parks and amusement rides. Ferrari World in Abu Dhabi has the world's fastest—and some say, scariest—roller coaster. Wild

Money Facts

The basic currency in the United Arab Emirates is the dirham, which is made up of 100 fils. The dirham comes in both coins and notes. Coins are 1, 5, 10, 25, and 50 fils and 1 dirham. Banknotes come in 5, 10, 20, 50, 100, 200, 500, and 1,000 dirhams. The bills depict wildlife, buildings, and other items associated with the UAE. Each denomination has a different dominant color. For example, the 50-dirham note is predominantly purple. It shows an oryx on the front, and a sparrowhawk and al-Jahili Fort on the reverse. A falcon watermark appears on all banknotes to prevent the money from being counterfeited. In 2015, 3.87 dirhams equaled US$1.00.

The Mall of the Emirates in Dubai features a ski slope, where visitors can imagine they're in another part of the world.

Wadi Water Park in Dubai has water chutes, slides, and swimming. Shopping malls are vast. One mall even has an indoor ski slope. Tourism is the largest service sector in the UAE, providing jobs in parks, retail malls, restaurants, hotels, and local transportation.

Recognizing the desire for beachfront properties, Dubai has supported the building of several groups of islands in its local waters. These human-built islands sit on tons of stone and

concrete, and residents and visitors enjoy exclusive beaches along with the world's swankiest hotel, the Palm Jumeirah.

Dubai and Abu Dhabi have grown into regional financial centers. There are branches of fifty banks in Dubai. Abu Dhabi has an equal number of banks, and both emirates attract investment firms for businesses and individuals.

Retail sales are a major part of the service sector. The UAE is filled with everything from expensive car retailers to vegetable stalls in open air markets. There are many different souks, including one for gold and jewelry, and another for spices. Shopping is entertainment in the UAE. People can browse the souks, plan a day at an air-conditioned mall, or shop online. Even local supermarkets have begun to provide Internet shopping services. People may order online and have their groceries delivered to their homes.

Open for Business

Businesses in the UAE are open five days a week, but the days off are different from those most workers get off in the United States. Friday is kept as a holy day, and all businesses and schools are closed Friday and possibly Saturday. Some businesses also close at prayer times throughout the week.

Transportation

Most workers in the UAE travel to and from work on public transportation. Taxis work day and night. The fare in the daytime is half the cost of the fare at night. Expect a wild ride—taxi drivers earn money by carrying as many fares as possible in a day. They may not appreciate short trips, and some hurry the ride in order to get another, better fare.

Taxis are the most common form of public transportation in Dubai.

Driving in the UAE is often dangerous. The UAE has the highest rate of road fatalities in the Middle East, and one of the highest in the world. In the UAE, traffic fatalities account for more deaths each year than diseases do. In an effort to get from one place to another, drivers weave in and out of traffic, slam on their brakes, speed in and out of traffic circles at breakneck paces, and ignore traffic laws. Inner lanes on highways are reserved for speed demons traveling at 120 miles per hour (200 kph).

Roads between cities have unmarked speed bumps that, when taken at great speed, cause cars to fly and stomachs to heave. Other highway dangers include shifting sand dunes and camels on the roads. There are no "Beware of Camel" signs. UAE drivers just expect to meet one or a dozen as they travel.

Drivers share the road with camels—and blowing sand.

CHAPTER 7

People of the Emirates

RASHID'S CIVICS TEACHER REQUIRES HIS STUDENTS to produce a population map of the United Arab Emirates. This sounds simple enough, but Rashid is running into a few problems. If his teacher wants the population of Emirati citizens, the population will be quite small and not represent the true population of his country. Emiratis make up less than one-fifth of the nation's total population. If Rashid focuses on the total population of the UAE, he will have an even greater problem. Which figure is correct? It is a difficult question.

Opposite: **A group of Emiratis and foreigners attend a parade celebrating National Day.**

The UAE Population

The population of the UAE is changing constantly. The total number of people in the UAE is always a guess. The population increases by thousands of people when a major construction project is underway, and then decreases once the people leave after the project ends. Winter populations are higher than summer populations, when it is too hot to work outside.

The Bedu

Almost all Emirati citizens can trace their heritage back to the Bedu or Bedouin people, the traditional nomads of the desert. Once, the Bedu were camel herders, living in goatskin tents and traveling between oases or wadis where rain had fallen. Today, only about 10 percent of Bedouin live in the traditional nomadic way. Instead, most live in small towns and suburbs and travel in four-wheel-drive vehicles rather than riding camels.

Among Emirati citizens, the population is growing at more than 1 percent a year. Emiratis, however, made up only an estimated 16 percent of the country's total population in 2009. The UAE is full of immigrants. Many of these foreigners come from South Asian countries such as India and Pakistan. Most provide labor for the construction and petroleum industries, although many work in hotels or restaurants or as household employees.

The population of men is more than twice that of women. In 2015, an estimated 6.6 million males and 2.9 million females lived in the UAE. The male population is so much larger than the female population because of the many working-class men who have immigrated to the UAE.

City and Country

Eighty-five percent of people in the UAE live in cities. One reason that such a high rate of urban living exists is because the rural areas of the UAE are mostly desert. Cities are also

Ethnicity in the UAE (2009 est.)	
South Asian	58%
Other (including Iranian and Southeast Asian)	17%
Emirati	16%
Western	9%

where the government builds housing. There are some small towns near oases.

Living within a city such as Dubai means having electricity, air-conditioning, transportation, a variety of foods readily available, and facilities such as schools, hospitals, and libraries. People in outlying areas usually rely on wells for water. They may or may not have electricity, and may raise sheep, goats, or chickens along with vegetables to add to their food supply. Today, with online shopping, rural dwellers can shop for and have delivered nearly anything they need.

Investing in Education

In 1975, half the men in the UAE could read and write. For women, only one in three was literate. At the time, the UAE had very little money to invest in education programs. Then, the price of oil rose, and the UAE became wealthy. Sheikh Zayed, the UAE's first president, said, "The greatest use that can be made of wealth is to invest it in creating generations of educated

Population of Largest Cities (2010 est.)	
Dubai	2,174,000
Abu Dhabi	1,500,000
Sharjah	543,733
Al-Ain	408,733
Ajman	226,172

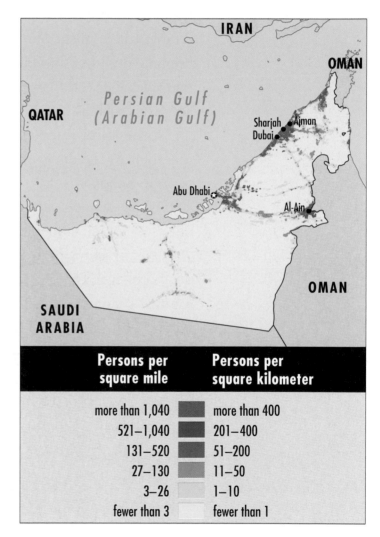

Persons per square mile	Persons per square kilometer
more than 1,040	more than 400
521–1,040	201–400
131–520	51–200
27–130	11–50
3–26	1–10
fewer than 3	fewer than 1

and trained people." The sheikh funded new schools and skills training, and today 90 percent of men and women are literate.

Primary school is free to everyone, and all children are required to attend school from ages six through twelve. Kindergarten in the UAE prepares children to begin their school careers. Children learn how to work together, and they begin English studies. All Emirati students learn both Arabic and English. The course of study is similar to schools in England and the United States. Classes include social studies, math, science, and language arts. There are also after-school activities such as soccer and basketball.

In the lower primary classes, girls and boys attend school together. In the upper grades, young men and women attend separate schools.

Private schools are found in every large city. About four out of every ten students in the nation attend private school.

After finishing high school, many young Emiratis continue on to college. The government pays for higher education for Emirati students. Non-Emiratis pay fees for college. Ninety-five percent of girls and 80 percent of boys in their final years of school apply for college. The UAE has three public colleges: United Arab Emirates University, Zayed University, and Higher Colleges of Technology. There are also private colleges and universities, such as Ajman University of Science and Technology, American Universities of Sharjah, and American University in Dubai. Women make up 79 percent of the student body at UAE University, and more than 10,000 women attend the Higher Colleges of Technology.

Students attend class at a private French school in Dubai.

Language

The official language of the United Arab Emirates is Arabic. This language uses the Arabic alphabet, which is read from right to left. The letters are in a curving script. Arabic calligraphy is quite beautiful and is considered an art form.

Classical Arabic is based on the language used in the Qur'an. Modern writers, however, rarely use the classical form of Arabic. Instead, they use what is called Modern Standard Arabic, which is much easier. In the UAE, the form of Arabic spoken is called Gulf Arabic. The same dialect is spoken in parts of Saudi Arabia, Kuwait, Qatar, and Bahrain.

The English language borrows many words from Arabic. The mathematical terms *algebra* and *algorithm* come from Arabic, as do the words *candy*, *coffee*, *lemon*, *sherbet*, *sofa*, and *mattress*.

CHAPTER 8

The Path of Islam

I T IS 4:30 A.M., AND THE WAILING OF THE *AZAN* BURSTS forth from the minaret. It is the call to prayer. Maryam yawns and rises from her bed. She washes and prepares for her day. Every day begins the same. The azan calls, *"Allah-u Akbar"*—"God is great." It is the beginning of prayer. Maryam must complete her prayers before sunrise.

Maryam has a prayer rug facing Mecca. She uses it at home, and she has a prayer room at work, where she prays with the other women at her office.

Opposite: **The Sheikh Zayed Grand Mosque in Abu Dhabi is the largest mosque in the UAE. Its main prayer hall can hold seven thousand people, and all the spaces in the mosque put together can accommodate forty thousand worshippers.**

Daily Prayer

Muslims pray five times a day. The first prayer is just before dawn. Other prayer times are when the sun is directly overhead, when the sun is in a position to create shadows the same length as the person casting the shadow, at sunset, and at nightfall. The timing of these prayers changes daily as the seasons change. Prayer times are printed in newspapers and posted in mosques.

Religion in the UAE*	
Muslim	76%
Christian	13%
Hindu	7%
Buddhist	2%
Baha'i	1%

*Numbers do not equal 100% because of rounding

Some Muslims pray daily at a mosque, but it is not necessary. The time of prayer is important, but the place does not matter. All a Muslim needs for prayer is to know the direction of Mecca. In the UAE, all public buildings, ceilings in hotels, and offices have arrows indicating the direction of Mecca. Many workplaces and public buildings have prayer rooms for men and women. In the cities, there are mosques in every neighborhood.

The Beginnings of Islam

The Prophet Muhammad (ca. 570–632) was born in Mecca, in what is now Saudi Arabia. At age forty, Muhammad reported that the angel Gabriel visited him and revealed to him the word of God. Muhammad believed that "God Is One" and to surrender life to God is the only acceptable way to live.

A *qiblah* (also spelled qeblah) arrow points in the direction of Mecca, Saudi Arabia.

A woman reads the Qur'an at a mosque in Dubai.

Islam literally means "surrender." The Prophet met resistance, but he continued preaching. He and his followers moved from Mecca to Medina in 622.

The revelations Muhammad is said to have received from God make up the verses of the Qur'an. It is the main source of Muslim belief, setting down rules for life. When Emiratis speak to each other, there are two phrases that are often heard: *al-hamdu lillah* (thanks be to God) and *insha'allah* (God willing).

Each year, millions of Muslims make a pilgrimage to the Grand Mosque in Mecca, Saudi Arabia, where they perform many rituals. These include circling a cube-shaped structure called the Kaaba, which is said to hold a stone given to Adam, whom Muslims believe was the first man on earth.

The Five Pillars of Islam

There are five duties that every Muslim should follow. These are known as the five pillars of Islam. First, there is *shahada*, a public declaration of faith, which states, "There is no god but God, and Muhammad is the messenger of God." The second pillar is *salat*, the ritual prayer performed each day.

The third pillar is *zakat*, which is giving aid to the poor. Muslims are expected to give one-fortieth of their annual income to those in need. The fourth pillar is *sawm*, which is fasting (not eating) from sunrise to sunset during the month of Ramadan. The final pillar, *hajj*, is a call for all Muslims to make a pilgrimage to Mecca at least once in a lifetime if they are physically and financially able.

The Hijri Calendar

Muslims follow the Hijri calendar, which is based on the lunar year. This calendar counts years beginning in 622 CE, the year Muhammad fled Mecca for Medina. For example, the year 2020 is the year 1398 according to the Hijri calendar.

Because the Hijri is a lunar calendar, meaning it is based on the appearance of the moon, it is eleven days shorter than the Western calendar. This means that Muslim holidays fall on different days of the Western calendar from year to year.

Islam also guides Muslims in other ways. Muslims are forbidden to eat pork. They are not supposed to drink alcohol. People are expected to behave respectfully and with dignity and to dress modestly.

Men enjoy a meal in a mosque in Dubai after sundown during Ramadan.

Religious Holidays

Dates of Muslim holidays vary from year to year on the
Western calendar, so dates are not included below.

Prophet Muhammad's Birthday

Isra and Miraj Night

Ramadan

Eid al-Fitr

Hajj Season

Eid al-Adha

Hijri New Year

Islamic Celebrations

The most important religious time for Muslims is Ramadan.
For the entire month of Ramadan, all adult Muslims, except
for the sick, the elderly, and pregnant women, are expected to
fast during the day. They take no food or water from sunrise to
sunset. At sundown, Muslims break their fast with a large family dinner. The month is dedicated to sacrifice, reflection, and
practicing self-control. Ramadan is also a time to be generous
and to give to charity.

Hajj season is the time when pilgrims head to Mecca. *Hajj*
literally means "striving to reach a goal," and for Muslims, the
goal is to meet the obligation to reach Mecca. When Emiratis
travel to Mecca, they join millions of Muslims from throughout the world in professing their faith. The trip is symbolic.
Pilgrims participate in several rituals that reenact great stories
from their religion, such as the journey of Adam and Eve from
the Garden of Eden.

Other Religions

The UAE constitution declares that all people living in the Emirates are free to follow their religion of choice. But all Christians living in the UAE are foreigners. There are no Emirati Christians.

On the one hand, the UAE government does allow Christians, Buddhists, Hindus, and people of other faiths to practice their religions. But while foreigners are allowed to bring

Catholics attend mass in a church in Abu Dhabi. An estimated quarter million foreigners in the UAE are Catholic.

Bibles and other religious materials into the UAE, they are not allowed to promote Christianity among Emiratis. Conversion from Islam to any Christian faith is not allowed. Christian men are not allowed to marry Muslim women, and Christian women who marry Muslim men must convert to Islam.

Church buildings are welcome in the UAE. In fact, in 1998, the Dubai government donated land for the building of a church to be shared by four Protestant faiths and one group of Roman Catholics. Churches are limited, though, in how they may present their buildings. The churches cannot have bell towers or

Saint Mary Greek Orthodox Church in Dubai also serves people of other Christian faiths.

steeples with crosses on top. Also, churches cannot put crosses or other Christian symbols on the outside of their buildings. This includes crosses at Easter and at Nativity scenes at Christmas.

Many people living in the UAE practice Buddhism or Hinduism. There are estimated to be more than two hundred thousand Buddhists in the United Arab Emirates. As many as one million Indians are thought to live and work in the UAE. Many of them are Hindus.

Hindus pray in a temple in Dubai.

Digging Up a Church

Fourteen hundred years ago and before Islam came to the land of the UAE, monks built a Christian monastery at Sir Bani Yas Island in Abu Dhabi. Built around 600 CE, the monastery housed about forty monks. Efforts to uncover the monastery began in 1992. Although they cannot say for sure, experts believe the monks were members of the Nestorian Church, a Christian sect from western Asia. Archaeologists do know that the entire church was built around a tomb of one man. Archaeologists found rooms with plaster crosses hanging on the walls, and pottery bowls, jars, and glass bottles.

CHAPTER 9

A Rich and Varied Culture

MAHRA AL-SHAMSI RUBS DOWN HER HORSE, singing to it or reciting verses from the Qur'an. She is training for a desert endurance race. Her horse is named Miracle, and surviving the endurance race is a miracle in itself. Born and raised in a desert area near Ras al-Khaimah city, al-Shamsi has been entering endurance races for several years.

Endurance racing is fairly new as a regulated sport, but Bedouin riders have been holding races like this for centuries. A typical race is 35, 50, or 60 miles (60, 80, or 100 km) through the desert. The race tests both the rider and the horse, and al-Shamsi takes great care of her mounts. Both rider and horse need to be fit. The race is long, hot, and dusty, but thrilling for the riders. It is also part of the culture and heritage of the Emiratis. In the past, endurance rides across the desert tested the skill and stamina of Bedouin warriors.

Opposite: **Competitors take part in an endurance horse race through the desert.**

A Sporting Tradition

Traditional sports are highly valued in Emirati life. These sports include camel racing, horse racing, hunting with Saluki dogs, and falconry—all related to traditional Bedouin activities. The Bedouin hunted for food and practiced horse and camel skills for use in battles. Camel races used to be held on special occasions, such as after a wedding. Today's camel races are well-organized events, held October through March. The camels race around the dusty track to the cheering of the

Young boys used to serve as jockeys in camel races, but the practice has been banned in the UAE because it is too dangerous for children. Today, small, sophisticated robots serve as camel jockeys.

crowd. Horse racing, equestrian events, and horse endurance races can also be traced back to Bedouin times. The UAE is home to world-class stables and breeding farms.

Hunting with Salukis is a pastime with a thousand-year heritage. The dogs were raised in desert environments and were trained by Bedouin people to find food. The Salukis are native to Yemen and are named for the Bani Saluk people. A pack of trained dogs can bring down an oryx or run down a gazelle. Another traditional hunting sport that survives today is falconry. Falconers catch and train their birds to hunt bustards, grouse, and pheasants. Once a way to get food, falconry is now a skilled sport that requires many hours of training for both bird and handler.

Salukis are one of the fastest dog breeds in the world. They can run 40 miles per hour (65 kph) and have great stamina.

Olympic Champion

As of 2015, Sheikh Ahmed bin Hasher al-Maktoum (1963–) is the only Emirati to have won an Olympic medal. He won a gold medal in the double trap event at the 2004 Olympics. In this event, competitors shoot at targets launched into the air. Sheik Ahmed is a member of the ruling family of Dubai. An avid sportsman, he was also a squash champion.

Modern Sports

Many Emiratis love sports. The local soccer league fills stadiums with men clad in the colors of their favorite teams. Soccer stars such as Adnan al-Talyani are popular role models for budding players. Cricket players head to the field with bat and ball. People from all walks of life go skiing and snowboarding all year. How are snow sports possible in Dubai, where the temperature frequently tops 100°F (38°C)? There, people can walk into a mall that has a snow park.

Team sports draw players and spectators to parks and arenas throughout the UAE. The professional soccer league has a dozen teams, and competition is fierce. Local soccer teams for youth are common in the cities. Dubai also has a club for rugby, which is a rough-and-tumble game similar to American football. Shooting is another team sport that requires plenty of practice. The Jebel Ali shooting club offers a high-tech experience in a firearms simulator room.

Water sports are popular, particularly since the UAE has such beautiful beaches and seas. Sailboarding, sailing, swimming, and scuba diving are enjoyed all year round. The weather is warm, and the waters are a welcome relief from the desert heat.

Music and Dance

Throughout the UAE's history, people have enjoyed music and dance as a way of telling stories of their daily lives. Songs praised the warriors, pearl divers, and seafarers. Whether cooking, cleaning, rowing the dhows, or riding into battle, every event was accompanied by music or voices.

An Emirati player swings at a ball during a match between the UAE and Ireland in the Cricket World Cup in 2015.

Oud, Daf, and Rababa

When the music is traditional—and it usually is in the UAE—the instruments are traditional as well. The *oud* is a stringed instrument similar to a lute, with a pear-shaped base, a short neck, and angled pins to hold the strings. A *daf* is a tambourine that can be tapped for a drumlike sound or shaken for a rattling sound. A *rababa* (left) is also a stringed instrument with a small, round sounding board, a very narrow neck, and a bow. With a few drums added to the mix, a band is formed.

A Rich and Varied Culture   **105**

Emirati men perform a traditional dance.

At the end of a long day traveling across the desert, men gathered around campfires. They told stories and recited poems, many of which became the lyrics of traditional songs. Here are the lyrics of a folk song dealing with the women who waited for their men to return home from pearling:

Neighbor of mine, my adventurous sailor shall return.

Neighbor of mine, he shall return from the world of dangers.

With perfumes, precious stones, rose water, and incense, he shall return.

He shall return, and to see him again will be like seeing the moon.

The UAE has several radio stations that play a variety of music. Some stations play rock music, while others feature dance music or rhythm and blues. There are also talk radio stations. Broadcasts are under strict rules, and songs that have

One of the best-known singers and songwriters in the UAE is Hamdan al-Abri (1981 –), the front man for the band ABRI. The band has released two hit albums, *Sunchild* and *Blank Notes*. ABRI has toured the Middle East and is heard on the radio throughout the UAE. After the band broke up, Hamdan al-Abri went solo. Two of his singles have been featured on U.S. television shows and are popular in Europe.

rude content are not played. Broadcasts are made in Arabic, English, and Indian languages, such as Hindi and Malayalam.

Along with traditional music, the UAE has several dances that remind the dancers and their audiences of their Bedouin heritage. One of the most popular is the *ayyalah*, the sword dance. Performed by men armed with swords, the intense rhythm and athletic movements become increasingly dangerous as the men leap and twirl between drawn swords. This dance is often part of the entertainment at weddings.

Henna Tattoos

The complex lines and patterns of henna tattoos are called *mehndi* designs. Reddish-brown or black henna tattoos are drawn on hands, wrists, feet, and ankles. The tattoos are usually temporary, lasting a few weeks, but permanent henna tattoos are also available. In the United Arab Emirates, brides traditionally get elaborate henna tattoos for their weddings. Henna is also popular among tourists.

Arts and Crafts

The Emiratis proudly display the arts and crafts of their ancestors. Among the most remarkable works of art in the emirates is Arabic calligraphy. Arabic letters have soft curves and bold strokes. Art galleries and museums hang beautiful calligraphy of Qur'an texts or verse.

Other traditional Emirati art forms include jewelry making, woodcarving, rug making, and weaving. Emirati jewelry is generally gold. Jewelers incorporate pearls, amber, and other

Elaborate jewelry is for sale at the Dubai gold market.

gems into dramatic necklaces, cuff bracelets, and dangling earrings. Women use small handlooms to produce *al sadu* weaving, a woolen fabric used for robes and scarves.

Many adults in the UAE have handcrafted prayer rugs. These rugs are handed down through families and may be more than a hundred years old.

Fine arts are on display in the nation's many museums. Two of the world's great art museums—the Louvre in Paris, France, and the Guggenheim in New York City, have branch museums in the UAE. In addition, the cultural district on Saadiyat Island in Abu Dhabi features art from around the world. Saadiyat is also home to the Abu Dhabi Art Fair. Although the fair is relatively new, it draws painters and sculptors who attract large crowds.

The Written Word

Poetry is the most respected form of writing in the UAE. Emiratis read, write, and recite poetry at every event. UAE poetry may be romantic, patriotic, humorous, or religious in nature. Poets are highly respected for their skills. Adel Khozam is not only a poet, but also a journalist for *Banipal* magazine. Ousha the Poet is an award-winning female poet who has been honored at many literary events. Even some politicians are poets. Sheikh Zayed bin Sultan al-Nahyan and Sheikh

Adel Khozam is one of the many Emirati poets who have gained international attention in recent years.

Mohammed bin Rashid al-Maktoum have written *nabati* poetry, a traditional form written in Classical Arabic. Here is a bit of poetry by Sheikh Mohammed, the vice president and prime minister:

> The dark nights and hard days
> We take them as they come and worry not about the future.
> We walk along an unbeaten track
> And if the path is difficult I enjoy it more.

In the UAE, novels have not traditionally been as popular as poetry, but several Emirati writers are breaking the mold. Authors such as Alyazia al-Suwaidi and Sheikha al-Muhairi have made history by writing fantasy novels geared to teenaged readers. The idea of authors publishing fiction in the UAE has met with approval from attendees at the Abu Dhabi International Book Fair. In a workshop titled "Made in the UAE," authors and illustrators exhibited a wide range of children's books and young adult works. A key factor in all the books promoted is that each meets UAE cultural norms and features Emirati heroes.

This book fair is just one of many efforts to promote literature in the UAE. Kalima, a project in Abu Dhabi, arranges the translation and printing of popular literature into Arabic. The Sheikh Zayed Book Award is a yearly cash prize for authors and publishers who promote Arab literature. The ten-day Sharjah International Book Fair began in 1982. It is the oldest UAE event to promote literature. The fair's aim is to provide affordable, quality books to readers of all ages.

The Abu Dhabi International Book Fair features participants from more than fifty countries, offering books in more than thirty languages.

Performing Arts

The Abu Dhabi National Theatre is the center for performing arts in the UAE. The theater is large and modern, with an auditorium that seats more than two thousand people. The theater presents classical and pop musicians, operas, and dramas. A presentation of *Khalifa in Our Hearts*, an operetta of Arabic songs and poems, received rave reviews. Drama with universal themes is frequently presented. For example, an Arabic version of William Shakespeare's *Richard III*, set in today's Arabian Peninsula, was staged using a mainly Arab cast.

The Abu Dhabi National Theatre is one of the nation's leading cultural institutions.

Several programs provide opportunities for young performing artists. The Dubai Festival for Youth Theatre gives budding actors a place to test their skills. The Emirates Youth Symphony Orchestra encourages young musicians interested in playing classical music.

Although few movies are made in the UAE, the nation hosts several film festivals. UAE movie theaters show Hollywood blockbusters, Indian feature films, action films, thrillers, dramas, and comedies. The films are current hits from throughout the world, many showing at the same time they are released in the United States, Canada, or Europe. Films are presented in Arabic, English, Hindi, French, and Spanish. A night at the movies is a popular outing for many Emiratis.

The *zurna* is a common instrument used in traditional music in the United Arab Emirates.

A Rich and Varied Culture **113**

CHAPTER 10

Everyday Life

YASMINA IS ABOUT TO BE MARRIED. TWENTY-TWO years old, she has earned a college degree and teaches English at a local elementary school. Her life as a bride will be quite different from that of her mother and worlds apart from that of her grandmother.

Family Changes

In Yasmina's grandmother's day, parents arranged marriages. Yasmina's grandmother was her grandfather's second of four wives. In traditional Islam, men are allowed to have up to four wives if they can support them all equally. Grandmother went to live in the family compound along with her husband's parents, his two brothers and their wives, and more than fifty children. The house was divided in half, with women having their own sitting rooms, dining rooms, and bathing facilities.

Yasmina's mother married a distant cousin, a man she had met only twice in her life. She and her groom signed the marriage contract, known locally as the *milcha*, in her home. Her

Opposite: **On average, Emirati women are twenty-six years old when they get married.**

Emirati men relax before a wedding. Emirati men can receive a marriage grant from the government for up to 70,000 dirhams, which is worth about US$19,000, to pay for wedding expenses.

wedding party lasted three days, with men and women celebrating separately. Right after she married, Yasmina's mother moved into a compound with a large group of in-laws. Yasmina's parents divorced shortly after she was six. At that time, her father paid the required divorce allotment. Yasmina and her two younger siblings lived with her mother. Her older brother stayed with his father's family.

Today, Yasmina will marry a man she chose herself. She met her groom at work and then had a cousin arrange a meeting between both sets of parents to promote the marriage. Yasmina and Khalim will be married in Sharjah in a group of more than twenty couples. They will have one huge reception and one dinner feast. Much of the cost will be paid for by the government marriage fund. Set up in 1994, the marriage fund pays a grant for weddings. Yasmina was able to arrange for their marriage grant and health exam online. She was also able to join a wedding collective, purchase her dress, and arrange for their new house on the Internet as well. She and Khalim, being native Emiratis, are entitled to a new house supplied by the government. Yasmina plans to continue teaching. It is a new world in Sharjah for young, educated women.

From Birth to Death

The birth of a child is a celebration in every UAE family. Because family is so important, couples tend to have many children, and each child is immediately registered in the Family Book. This

In 1990, Emirati women had an average of 4.4 children over the course of their lifetimes. Today, that rate has fallen to 2.4.

book lists the details of the birth, the child's name, and the parents' names. Being listed in the Family Book is essential because without that listing the child is not an Emirati citizen.

When a newborn comes home, the child is wrapped in a white cloth that is tied around the baby with a crocheted string. Visitors to the family tuck money under the string. Both sides of the family honor the baby, but every child is known as the father's child. The newborn gets a name that includes his or her father's name and his or her father's family name.

As children grow, they continue to live with their parents. Upon reaching the age of seven or eight, boys join their fathers in the male half of the house. Girls stay with their mothers.

In their teen years, young Emiratis are not allowed to date. They do go out with friends and keep in touch with everyone through cell phones, texting, and social media. When girls reach puberty, they begin wearing an *abaya* (a long robe) and *shayla* (a headscarf).

The younger generation of adults is expected to care for their parents as the parents age. This is easily done if they all live in the same compound. If they do not, then a visit once a week on Friday is the least that is expected of the children. When a parent dies, there are many rituals that must be performed.

The body must be washed and wrapped in white cloth. It is common that burial is on the same day as the death. This is a practical custom, since bodies decay rapidly in hot weather. The oldest son plans the funeral, and both sons and sons-in-law carry the body to the cemetery for burial. Every man attending the funeral throws a handful of soil on the coffin. The men

then gather at the home of a male family member. The death is mourned for three days between afternoon and evening prayers. Women do not participate in the funeral, although they do have a three-day mourning period, also between afternoon and evening prayers. They do their mourning in the women's section of the home. In both groups, verses from the Qur'an are read in memory of the deceased and to support the remaining family members.

More than one out of every five people in the United Arab Emirates is under the age of fifteen.

What's for Dinner?

In an Emirati household, breakfast means eggs. The eggs are accompanied by salty white cheese, a glass of buttermilk or *labneh* (yogurt, water, and mint), and bread. Sometimes there are lentils in garlic sauce, and other times there may be *ful medames*, a bean dish with olive oil. The bread, called *khobz*,

Workers make flatbread at a bakery in Dubai.

may be any one of forty different varieties of bread, but is most likely something similar to pita bread, which can be torn off and used to scoop up food.

Lunch is some combination of rice and protein. The rice may be plain or laced with whole cardamom pods or with raisins. It is served over a meat stew with chicken, lamb, goat, or camel. When not stewed, the meat is grilled or roasted. The UAE's access to fresh seafood means that along the coast, lamb or goat are replaced with the catch of the day. Common fish dishes are grouper, mullet, kingfish, or tuna, grilled or roasted and served with lemon, lime, cabbage, and rice.

In the UAE, families sometimes have the same trouble getting together for family dinner as Western families do. Many teens have snacked on a burger and fries after school and have homework to do. Their younger brothers and sisters might get impatient for dinner and be given bread and cheese or cake to tide them over. Wives might have picked up a sandwich or kebab at a restaurant, husbands would rather eat with their friends at a coffeehouse, and grandmother has perhaps been munching all afternoon on dates and *halwah*, a candy made from sesame seeds and honey. If the family does eat together, the males eat with other males, and the females eat with other females.

Many UAE residents like to go out to dinner. In UAE cities, a diner can get every type of food imaginable, so it is not unusual for people to dine on Chinese noodles one night, Mongolian stir-fry the next, and Greek spanakopita the night after. Lebanese food is popular because restaurants offer free appetizers of spiced spinach leaves, ripe melon, cheese, artichokes, and olives. Stands

In 2015, there were 128 McDonald's restaurants in the United Arab Emirates.

selling American-style burgers and fried chicken are next to stalls selling falafel (balls of fried chickpeas).

Popular beverages include camel milk, yogurt drinks, and delicious fresh fruit juices. Drinking tea is an experience. The scalding-hot brew is poured from about 3 feet (1 m) above the glass. Emiratis like their tea extremely sweet. Many men spend afternoons sipping a cup of strong coffee at a coffee-house, chatting with friends or reading the paper. There are also coffee shops where both men and women can buy a cold beverage, roasted chicken, tabouleh (a salad featuring parsley, tomatoes, and bulgur wheat), and fresh fruit.

The UAE is one of the top ten countries in the world that consume the most tea per person.

UAE-Style Hummus

Hummus is a popular dip served with fresh, warm pita bread. Although you can buy it at the store, nothing beats the flavor of fresh, homemade hummus. Have an adult help you with this recipe.

Ingredients

¼ cup lemon juice

¼ cup tahini (sesame seed paste)

1 clove garlic, small, peeled, and minced

2 tablespoons olive oil

¾ teaspoon salt

¼ teaspoon ground pepper

½ teaspoon ground cumin

1 can garbanzo beans, 15 ounces, drained

2 tablespoons water

Fresh pita bread

Directions

Combine the lemon juice and the tahini in a food processor. Process for 1 minute, and then scrape the sides of the bowl and process for another minute. The mixture should be very smooth. Add the garlic, olive oil, salt, pepper, and cumin to the lemon juice mixture and process for another 30 seconds. Scrape the sides of the bowl and process again for 30 seconds. The mixture should be very smooth.

Drain the garbanzo beans. Add $\frac{1}{3}$ of the beans to the food processor and process until smooth (about 1 minute). Repeat this process twice more, so that all the beans have been used. Be sure to scrape the sides between each addition to ensure the mixture stays smooth. Add 2 tablespoons of water, and process 1 minute.

Place the hummus in a small bowl. Wrap pita bread in foil and heat in the oven at 250°F for 5 minutes. Cut the bread into triangles. Serve the hummus with the pita on the side.

What to Wear

Although the UAE has a hot climate, people typically wear long clothing. One reason for this is that the clothing keeps sweat close to the body, so people do not lose dangerous amounts of water. The long clothing also keeps the sun's rays off the skin, helping to cool it. The style of dress also follows Islam, which urges people to dress modestly. "Modest dress" can be interpreted in many different ways, but in the UAE people usually cover their arms and legs entirely.

Emirati women typically wear an *abaya*, a long, flowing robe that completely covers the body. An everyday abaya may be perfectly plain, but for special events many women have abayas with jeweled designs. Under the abaya, many women wear dresses or pants, which cannot be seen. Many women wear a *shayla*, a piece of material used to cover the hair. This scarf may be black or colorful, and some women wear designer scarves that match the handbags they carry.

A shayla should not be confused with a *burqa*, which is a head cover with a slit for the eyes. Most women who wear a burqa also have a metallic section covering the lower part of the face. Usually, only elderly women wear burqas. There are two other types of head coverings, a *gishwa* and a *hijab*. The gishwa is a thin, black veil for covering the face. The wearer can see through the gishwa, but other people cannot see the woman's face. The hijab is designed to cover the hair, but it is rarely worn in the UAE.

Traditionally, Emirati men wear a long, loose robe called a *kandura*. The kandura is usually white, but in the winter dark kanduras are sometimes worn. A long robe indicates high social status. A short robe represents someone in a lower social status. Men also wear a head covering called a *ghutra*. This is a square of white or checkered cotton, draped loosely over the head. The ghutra is held in place by an *iqal*. Ropelike in appearance, an *iqal* is usually black.

Festivals and Holidays

Because the UAE is a Muslim nation, and Islam is the state religion, many national holidays are also religious holidays. Although Ramadan is an important time, it is not considered a holiday. People fast during the day, but they still go to work

Like their fathers, many young boys wear long, white kanduras.

Emiratis gather to pray during Eid al-Fitr.

and school. Work hours are usually shortened out of consideration for those fasting. Hajj is also a religious event that is not a public holiday. At the end of these events, however, people are ready to have a good time.

Eid al-Fitr is a three-day festival that celebrates breaking the fast at the end of Ramadan. People dress up, families eat together, and children get treats. The feast extends to the poor, and families make a point of feeding those in need. The celebration is not to cheer for the end of fasting. It is to celebrate the gift God gives that allows Muslims to participate in Ramadan.

Eid al-Adha comes at the end of hajj season and honors those who have made pilgrimages. As part of the celebration, families have a sheep, camel, or goat slaughtered. This recalls the story of Abraham being willing to sacrifice his son because God told him to. The purpose is not to kill animals but to show a willingness to make sacrifices to God. The families do not slaughter the animals at home. They arrange for a local farm to provide the animal and slaughter it humanely. Families give one-third of the meat of the slaughtered animal to friends and one-third to the poor. They keep the final one-third to feast on.

In the UAE, people celebrate two New Years. The first comes at the beginning of the lunar year. This date changes on the Western calendar from year to year. The other New Year is the same one celebrated around the world on January 1.

UAE citizens celebrate every holiday with song, dance, and feasting. They enjoy family and friends, but there is always an awareness of their responsibilities as Muslims. In the midst of every celebration, people find time to feed the poor and help the needy. There is an ever-present sense of the tenets of the Muslim faith, which weaves a path through all aspects of Emirati life.

UAE National Day

National Day honors the establishment of the UAE in 1971. The holiday is celebrated with fireworks, concerts, and a grand parade. A car and bike parade features vintage, exotic, and extraordinarily expensive cars. There are bike stunts, a soccer marathon, a fashion show, and art exhibitions. In 2015, one hundred graffiti artists created a scroll 1.2 miles (2 km) long at Jumeirah Beach Park.

Timeline

UAE HISTORY

Abu Dhabi and Sharjah become pearling centers.	**ca. 5500 BCE**
Al-Ain becomes a stop on trade routes.	**ca. 2000 BCE**
The Umayyads bring Arabic and Islam to the UAE region.	**600s CE**
The United Kingdom and the emirates sign a treaty to end violence on the seas.	**1820**
A treaty gives Great Britain responsibility for defense and foreign relations in the emirates.	**1892**

WORLD HISTORY

ca. 2500 BCE	The Egyptians build the pyramids and the Sphinx in Giza.
ca. 563 BCE	The Buddha is born in India.
313 CE	The Roman emperor Constantine legalizes Christianity.
610	The Prophet Muhammad begins preaching a new religion called Islam.
1054	The Eastern (Orthodox) and Western (Roman Catholic) Churches break apart.
1095	The Crusades begin.
1215	King John seals the Magna Carta.
1300s	The Renaissance begins in Italy.
1347	The plague sweeps through Europe.
1453	Ottoman Turks capture Constantinople, conquering the Byzantine Empire.
1492	Columbus arrives in North America.
1500s	Reformers break away from the Catholic Church, and Protestantism is born.
1776	The U.S. Declaration of Independence is signed.
1789	The French Revolution begins.
1865	The American Civil War ends.
1879	The first practical lightbulb is invented.

UAE HISTORY		WORLD HISTORY	
		1914	World War I begins.
		1917	The Bolshevik Revolution brings communism to Russia.
		1929	A worldwide economic depression begins.
The pearling industry begins to decline.	1930s		
		1939	World War II begins.
		1945	World War II ends.
Oil is discovered in Abu Dhabi.	1958		
Oil is discovered in Dubai.	1966		
		1969	Humans land on the Moon.
The United Arab Emirates is formed; Sheikh Zayed bin Sultan al-Nahyan becomes the first president.	1971		
		1975	The Vietnam War ends.
		1989	The Berlin Wall is torn down as communism crumbles in Eastern Europe.
		1991	The Soviet Union breaks into separate states.
		2001	Terrorists attack the World Trade Center in New York City and the Pentagon near Washington, D.C.
Sheikh Zayed dies; Sheikh Khalifa becomes president.	2004	2004	A tsunami in the Indian Ocean destroys coastlines in Africa, India, and Southeast Asia.
Plans are drawn up to build a zero carbon footprint city, called Masdar.	2005		
The UAE holds its first elections ever.	2006		
A global financial crisis halts the real estate explosion in Dubai.	2008	2008	The United States elects its first African American president.
The Burj Khalifa tower opens in Dubai as the world's tallest building.	2010		
The UAE outlaws criticism of the government and protests through social media.	2012		
Some members of Al-Islah are imprisoned for planning to overthrow the government.	2013		

Fast Facts

Official name: United Arab Emirates

Capital: Abu Dhabi

Official language: Arabic

Abu Dhabi

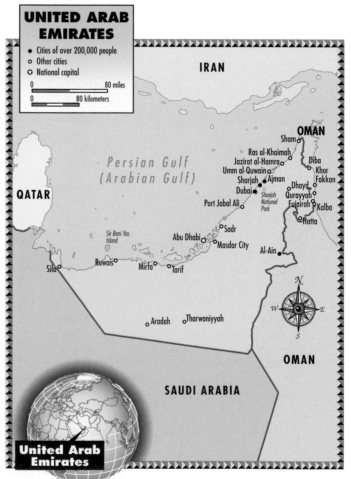

National flag

Mount Yibir

Official religion:	Islam
Date of founding:	December 2, 1971
National anthem:	"Ishy Bilady" ("Long Live My Nation")
Government:	Federation of emirates
Head of state:	President
Head of government:	Prime minister
Area of country:	32,278 square miles (83,600 sq km)
Latitude and longitude:	24.47° N, 54.37° E
Bordering countries:	Saudi Arabia to the south, Oman to the east
Highest elevation:	Mount Yibir, 5,010 feet (1,527 m) above sea level
Lowest elevation:	Sea level along the coast
Length of coastline:	819 miles (1,318 km)
Longest river:	There are no rivers.
Average high temperature:	In Dubai, 75°F (24°C) in January, 105°F (41°C) in July
Average low temperature:	In Dubai, 58°F (14°C) in January, 86°F (30°C) in July
Average annual rainfall:	4 to 6 inches (10 to 15 cm)

Burj Khalifa

**National population
(2015 est.):** 9,445,624

**Population of major
cities (2010 est.):**

Dubai	2,174,000
Abu Dhabi	1,500,000
Sharjah	543,733
Al-Ain	408,733
Ajman	226,172

Landmarks:
- ▶ *Burj Khalifa*, Dubai
- ▶ *Liwa Oasis*, Abu Dhabi
- ▶ *Palm Jumeirah*, Dubai
- ▶ *Sir Bani Yas*, Abu Dhabi
- ▶ *Souk al-Markazi*, Sharjah

Economy: Oil and natural gas are the largest part of the UAE's economy, accounting for about one-quarter of all the income generated. In recent years, the nation's economy has grown more diverse. Tourism, banking, and trade are now important. Manufacturing is growing, producing goods such as aluminum, steel products, wood products, plastics, chemicals, food products, and textiles. Major agricultural products include dates, melons, tomatoes, mangoes, cauliflower, eggplants, citrus fruits, chickens, and milk.

Currency: Dirham. In 2015, 3.87 dirhams equaled US$1.00.

**System of weights
and measures:** Metric system

Literacy rate (2012): 90%

Currency

Schoolchildren

Sheikh Khalifa bin Zayed
al-Nahyan

**Common Arabic
words and phrases:**

Ahlan, marhaban	Hello, welcome
Salam	Hi
Sabah el khair	Good morning
Masaa el khair	Good afternoon/evening
Ma'a salama	Good-bye
Kaifa haloka	How are you? (to a man)
Kaifa haloki	How are you? (to a woman)
Ana bekhair, wa anta?	I'm fine. And you? (to a man)
Ana bekhair, wa anti?	
	I'm fine. And you? (to a woman)
Shokran	Thank you
Btihki inglizi?/Teh ki ingleezi?	Do you speak English?

**Prominent
Emiratis:**

Adel Khozam (1963–)
Poet

Sheikh Ahmed bin Hasher al-Maktoum (1963–)
Olympic gold medalist in shooting

Sheikh Zayed bin Sultan al-Nahyan (1918–2004)
First president of the UAE

Sheikh Khalifa bin Zayed al-Nahyan (1948–)
President

Sheikha Lubna bint Khalid bin Sultan al-Qasimi (1962–)
First female minister in the UAE

Abdul Qader al-Rais (1951–)
Painter

Adnan al-Talyani (1964–)
Soccer player

To Find Out More

Books

- Ali-Karamali, Sumbul. *Growing Up Muslim: Understanding the Beliefs and Practices of Islam*. New York: Random House, 2013.

- Goldsworthy, Kaite. *Burj Khalifa with Code*. New York: Weigl Publications, 2012.

- McCoy, Lisa. *United Arab Emirates*. Broomall, PA: Mason Crest, 2010.

Music

- *Authentic World Series: Arabian Peninsula*. Nashville: Warner/Chappell, 2015.

- *The Rough Guide to Arabic Café*. London: World Music Network, 2008.

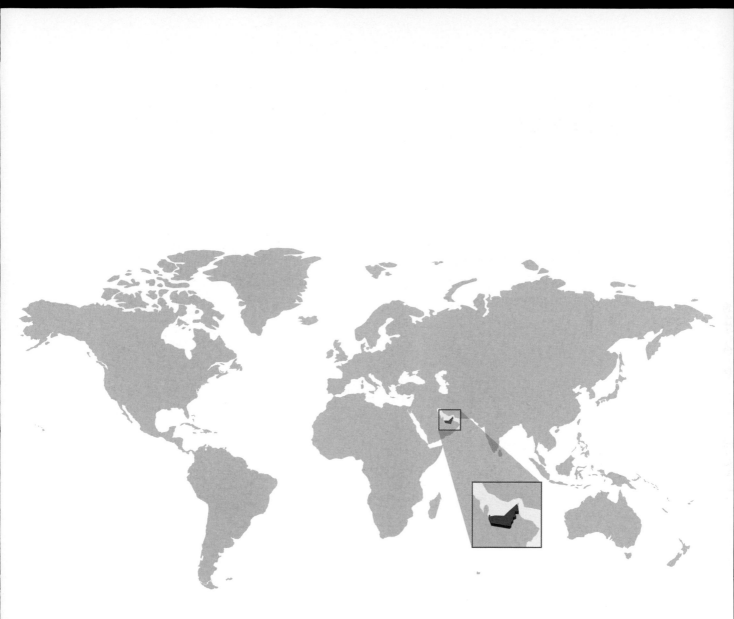

▶ Visit this Scholastic Web site for more information on United Arab Emirates:
www.factsfornow.scholastic.com
Enter the keywords **United Arab Emirates**

Index

Page numbers in *italics*
indicate illustrations.

Meet the Author

BARBARA SOMERVILL HAS BEEN writing children's nonfiction books for more than twenty years. She writes about countries, earth science, people, and social studies. Somervill teaches college writing and critical reading classes. When not teaching or writing, she loves going to the movies and theater, baking, and playing softball.

Photo Credits

7/16